LOVING LIFE AS IT IS

by Jennifer L. Manlowe, PhD

For my father
Robert Lewis Manlowe
November 23, 1935 – March 7, 2006

CONTENTS

Preface

During the years that I have been involved in Anonymous groups of Al-Anon (for the loved-one's of addicts), I have witnessed a huge increase in popular culture regarding addiction and its troubling effects on the lives of addicts and those living and working with them. All the big bookstores are devoting more and more shelf space to recovery and addiction materials. Articles appear daily on recovery and new insights on the biochemistry and psycho-social dynamics of addiction. Seemingly every other talk show host and their guests offer testimonials in support of Twelve Step programs that have transformed their lives. Even movies have been made that poke fun of the Twelve Step programs, like *28 Days* or *Safe*. Other movies, like *Changing Lanes, Clean and Sober,* and *Drunks* seem to silently recruit new members through showing the important "awakenings" that take place in Twelve Step meetings.[1]

So why another book when so much is already available on every kind of chemical and psychological addiction? How much more do we really need to understand? What could another book offer that has not already been said 1 million times before? And who am I to think I could add one more ounce of wisdom to the existing stack? I have wrestled with these questions for the past two years and yet I kept a daily journal, where I recorded reflections on my own "recovery" experience. I wrote down significant themes and images as they appeared in my meditations and dreams and recorded my ongoing efforts to reach a meaningful notion of a Higher Power—so necessary if one is to walk through the program of Twelve Steps Anonymous. Because I am a scholar of World Religions, I also documented a great deal of

---

[1] There is, of course, anti-12-step literature as well, see also the NY Times bestseller: *A Million Little Pieces* by James Frey.

myths and stories that I have encountered over the years in various religious traditions. Whether I was quoting a mystic, a rebel, a piece of Twelve Step program literature, or a world philosopher, I folded that wisdom into helping me understand the underlying philosophy of the Twelve-Step program, especially for someone like me…someone who vacillated between mates with their own addictions or returning to the drudgery of dealing with my own compulsion to use food and weight obsession to relieve anxiety.

Eventually, I began sharing material from my journal with other interested writers and friends. I also began giving workshops on "When *God* Doesn't Make Sense: Eastern Approaches to the Twelve Steps." In these workshops, I would help interested people—community activists, educators, mental health professionals, atheists, or curious agnostics—to explore how we "non-believers," (non-deists, really), can use the Twelve Steps to give us a non-egocentric or *spiritual* focus, without all that "God Talk."

The people who maintained an interest in what I had to say were often quite suspicious of Twelve Step programs and the things they had heard about "working the Steps." Ideas like "surrendering your life and will to the care of a God as you understand *Him*" gave both strong male and female friends pause; they had the urge to run the other way. Hearing me, a world philosophy professor, share my understanding and experience in the Twelve Step rooms proved helpful to many of them.

This book is intended for a wider audience than I have been able to reach in my small encounters with friends and workshops. I hope it provides a way to take the best of the Twelve Steps and the best of World Philosophies and weave them together to better understand the variety of ways "spiritual recovery" may be found. Working with life on life's terms is a necessity to more wisely work with our own and others limitations. Finding spiritual language that speaks to each of us is one way to find a viable way of life—in or outside the program of Twelve Steps Anonymous. My hope is that the reader will make use of the wisdom to be found here by experimenting with the exercises that are given after every chapter, entitled, *Making This Practice My Own*. Remember to "take what you like and leave the rest behind." There is no magic bullet for dealing with life, no matter what the rows of self-help literature say. All we can do is start right where we are and practice, practice, practice keeping our grip on life a loose one.

As a member of Anonymous Programs, I also wrestled with the idea of putting my full name on the book jacket, after all, I will be talking about the learning I have experienced in the rooms of Twelve Step Anonymous. One friend said, "Jennifer, you might want to keep your own anonymity by using only your first name in this book." For those unfamiliar with Twelve Step programs, let me explain. Alcoholics Anonymous and other Twelve Step programs are guided by Twelve Traditions that serve as principles for their governance, to protect the fellowships from various forms of pressure and political turmoil that often destroy organizations. At the same time, these Traditions remind members that certain attitudes and behaviors, including the belief that one can publicly hold herself out as an authority on recovery, can be harmful to the individual member.[2]

I want to make myself very clear on the outset that I am speaking for myself and myself alone when I speak about what I've learned from Anonymous meetings and literature. In no way do I speak for the program of Twelve Steps Anonymous. This book is my personal experience and orientation to the Twelve Steps of recovery. We all have to find our own way. As the Buddha spoke to his disciples from his deathbed, "Be a lamp unto yourselves." No author, sponsor, therapist, coach or Twelve Step program can give anyone all of the answers; they

---

[2] Philip Z., *A Skeptic's Guide to the 12 Steps* (Minneapolis: Hazelden, 1990), iii.

can only offer suggestions for tuning into the strength, hope, and wisdom each person must discern for themselves.

Acknowledgments

This book owes its existence to the creative collective in Atlanta, Georgia. This is an Anonymous Group of very talented musicians, painters, poets, and fiction and non-fiction writers with whom I've had the good fortune of meeting and working on a weekly or bimonthly basis since August 2001. Angela, Linnie, John, and Elizabeth, thank you.

Thanks, also, to *The Creative Consulting Consortium*. This is a group of Atlanta women with whom I've met on a weekly basis to offer spiritual support to one another as increasingly creative independent contractors. C.J., Debbie, Ellen, Nancy and Rhonda, this book could not have come together without such tremendous, unapologetic enthusiasm and encouragement. Thank you so much.

Outside readers and dear friends: Whitney Bennett, Danielle Doughman, Tracy Lawrence, Susan Karr Kuebler, Karen Carr, Jean Walton, Mary Cappello and Jay Matthews, Bruce Webb, David Bokman, Daniel McMillan and Thomas P. Murphy, your thoughtful feedback on the first draft of this book is greatly appreciated.

Introduction

"Looking deeply at life as it is
in the very here and now,
the practitioner dwells
in stability and freedom"—*Buddhist Sutra*

"The first act of love is to see this person or this object, this reality *as it truly is*. The second ingredient is equally important to see yourself *as you truly are....*"—*Anthony de Mello*

"We easily love people for who we wish they were, we grow to hate them for who they actually are!"—*Danielle D.*

I find it telling that the theme of my first Anonymous meeting in Atlanta happened to be about a songwriter feeling stuck. We all know that old sob story about writer's block. The brief reading from the Al-Anon literature for this particular meeting included a pitiful story about how badly the author wanted "to be famous by now." And I almost burst out with an identificatory chortle. "Truth is," I thought to myself, "all I can do to get relief from my own writer's block is to get myself to an Anonymous

13

meeting, read some psychology and Buddhism, and meditate on releasing old thinking that fuels my age-old depression. For now, that's where it is."

I am now able to laugh at my own oxymoronic wish to be like Oprah (albeit, without the world sponsoring my yo-yo dieting and weight obsession), while at the same time achieving release from all attachments like Tibetan Buddhist teacher, Pema Chodron. Alongside wanting to be wealthy, happy and carefree, I want freedom from all forms of materialism, even spiritual materialism—where one is narcissistically-preoccupied with *being good* or *spiritually fruitful* all the time. As I said in that very meeting, "I have to accept myself and the simple wisdom I have to learn/offer and not expect to get affirmation from one more publication or academic approbation. I need to be okay with *just being.*" This is funny to me now. Because I left that particular Al-Anon meeting, went straight to a nearby coffee shop and began writing this book. After admitting my fear of my own ordinariness—and after I finished reading a book like the one I wanted to write called, *Cool Water: Alcoholism, Mindfulness and Ordinary Recovery*, by William Alexander, a Buddhist and former alcoholic—my own writer's block (iceberg, really) began to *calve*—that is, chunk off and melt. I realized, "Hey, I can write a book like *Cool Water*, but, instead, I can speak to women and men who have found themselves too often the co-alcoholic or codependent one in the relationship. Those of us who too often feel powerless in the face of a loved-one's addiction or mental illness need help too!"

Because I am a scholar of world religions, I will be folding in texts and tales from each tradition that I hope will foster wisdom in living and loving well—on life's terms. Each tradition has elements to draw from which will affirm the following: the goodness of questioning given truths; the utility in challenging old answers about what the rational mind can produce; the critical thinking that we must use to scrutinize societal standards for "the good life" and "who is a moral person?"

Figures from the world traditions can be our guides. For instance, we can draw strength from the wise counsel of Krishna to Arjuna in the Bhagavad-Gita[3], the spiritual risk-taking of the Biblical heroes Job, Sarah, Hagar and Abraham, the magical faith of the Sufi[4] poet Rumi's unrelenting gratitude, the skillful interdependence of Daoist immortals like Chuangzi and Laozi, the generosity and open-hearted fearlessness of Buddhist female Bodhisattvas[5], and the relational-intimacy and

---

[3] An Indian poem composed between the 2nd century BCE and the 2nd century CE and incorporated into the Mahabharata. Presented as a dialogue between the warrior prince Arjuna and his divine charioteer Krishna, it stresses the importance of doing one's duty and of faith in Brahman.

[4] Sufism is the esoteric dimension of the Islamic faith, the spiritual path to mystical union with God. It is influenced by other faiths, such as Buddhism, and reached its peak in the 13th century. There are many Sufi orders, the best known being the dervishes.

[5] In Mahayana Buddhism (1st century C.E.), a bodhisattva is a person of either gender who, according to some sources, can morph into any creature who is able to reach nirvana but delays doing so out of compassion in order to save suffering beings.

responsibility fostered by Confucius. Finally, this work returns again and again to the philosophical principles of the Twelve-Step Programs of Alcoholic Anonymous and Al-Anon which encourage mantras such as: "turn it over," "let go," and "work with life on life's terms!"

Loving Life As It Is began as a book written for all who hunger for authentic communion with themselves and others. This book comes after writing two academic-audience focused books—the first one is called *Faith Born of Seduction: Sexual Trauma, Body Image and Religion* and the second one is called *The Gender Politics of HIV/AIDS in Women* (both published by NYU Press).

In the fall of 2001, I grew tired of writing for academics alone, of making sense to only seven other people (often friends of mine!). The philosophy that I cared about was not meant to intimidate, it was not impossible to understand.

As one friend, named CJ, reminds me, "Jennifer, the philosophy you love to teach and think about has *legs* on it." It follows that I would now write a book for a broader audience. "Why?" you ask. Because, I want to read a book that would reflect some of the struggles that I have had with working to love "life as it is" and believe many can be helped by the spiritual lessons that I have garnered from teaching World Religion classes since 1996.

"All religion begins with the cry *Help!*"
—*William James*

For years I stayed away from Twelve-Step groups because of the Santa-like "God-talk" that I mistrust for its paternalistic assumptions (see my first book, *Faith Born of Seduction*). I resisted the infantilizing idea of an "all-knowing, all-protecting, all-providing-**for-me**, father-in-the-sky-with-a-secret-plan-just-for-me" world view. As the Buddhist scholar Nishitani Kenji says, "If you haven't dropped off self-seeking, you haven't even begun the spiritual path. When you stop asking, 'What can religion can do **for me?**' you've just begun the walk."

After circling for years what Twelve-Steppers call, "The Program," I finally remained in my seat long enough to reap the community-bred grace and compassion that can be found there. What I'm starting to comprehend is this: to make *a good life*, begin to see clearly the lies that you have been told and continue to tell yourself—by family, fearful religious traditions, the dominant consumptive culture, etc.—as lies spun by hurt or anxious people. Then start to uncover the genuinely good human that you already are. Start to see the good friendships that can be made all around you. Uncover the "soft spot" as Tibetan Buddhist Chogyam Trungpa Rinpoche would say. Uncover the wounded-heart and begin to feel your capacity to give and receive with sincere generosity. There is a truly warm person within you buried under your mental armor, prickly-guard, or people-pleasing defenses. It is really there but needs communal help to uncover it. Like the first-century faith-community that unwraps the mummified Lazarus in the Christian

Gospel story, Anonymous members unwrap and nurture each other. They uncover and foster each member's sense of self- and communal-responsibility and then assist in the further unwrapping and freeing of the next new member of the group.

Making This Practice My Own:

I, _____, am willing to sit undisturbed for about 10" a day for 90 days. Use this space (below) to write down what you want to get out of reading a book like this at this time.

What in your life do you love **as it is**?

What do you wish would change?

Falling Apart or Coming Together

"The sages describe a Way that leads to a higher level of existence, one infinitely more desirable than the level in which most people conduct their lives. The mystical tradition does not offer therapy in the usual sense of the word, but achieving the goal of mysticism—experiencing the Real Self—is said to cure human suffering because its very basis is thereby removed."
—psychiatrist, *Arthur Deikman*

"If you push far enough toward any one extreme, you'll eventually reach its opposite."
—*Martha Beck*

I had been married to Richard, the German philosopher and prolific writer, for just over a month when the psychological games that I played to make myself feel secure in the relationship stopped working and I began unraveling. The source of my emotional devolution seemed to be about trying to keep up appearances of being capable and self-sustaining inside a daily, face-to-face relationship with Richard. It is one thing to date "on line," reveal ourselves in our most appealing, revealing poses

21

as commuter daters, but it's quite another thing to experience each other's neuroses in day-to-day interactions. The revelations that were once erotic and exciting come to feel awkward and irritating, like trying to undress in the same narrow, hall closet. Elbows seem to bump the other's eye, egos bruise by accident, and still, blame is sought. The façade of romantic bliss fades and cracks and we can only do so much to spackle over one area before the other side of the foundation springs a leak through a new fracture in what we thought would be a solid "'til-death-do-us-part" arrangement.

Both Richard and I came from highly conscientious, Roman Catholic families. We each were motivated to excel in school, athletics, and to sacrifice ourselves for spiritual validation. I had been questioning the values of such image-focused martyrdom since about 1985 and Richard was still driven at once to please and rebel against his Catholic parents and upbringing. On the one hand, he would achieve the highest honors in school and work, and, on the other, he would drink nightly until he passed out to blot out any memory of his human foibles and fragile hungers for connection, self-transcendence and true renewal.

I did a lot to free myself of the pinched feelings I had inside me born of the ever-widening chasm between Richard and myself. I looked for what I've heard Twelve-Steppers call a "geographical cure." Even though Richard and I were falling farther and farther apart, I thought moving would help function for both of us as emotional glue. I bought a new condominium in downtown Atlanta, Georgia. Because I used all my savings for the down-payment, I had Richard sign a post-nuptial agreement saying our home would be mine if we ever split up.

I thought a lot about whether I would be able to live with someone I was coming to perceive as an ever-expanding baby—ever regressing. Freud might see Richard as one who was always looking for "the breast" to suck or the self-transcendence of the oceanic feeling of the womb. Richard was even less unconscious of his family-of-origin-born pain than I was (due to the fact that I wasn't above seeking counsel). As a result of this willed-ignorance he became aggressively-narcissistic about earning every academic accolade possible. Richard complained every time I left the house to run an errand or see a friend as if I were severing this preternatural umbilical cord between us. I was coming to see that he too appeared to be equally dissatisfied with our different styles-of-living. He regarded my independence and intense need for balance as sophomoric and insecure. And I was not living well with his excess spending, drinking, and once-a-day binge eating. He said, "You've changed, you've become a drag! We used to have fun together, now it's all work, penny-pinching and drudgery!" I wondered to myself, "Is this the typical complaint of all newlyweds?"

Of course, all of the daily excesses in which Richard drowned himself was tempting to me as well, especially as we got to know each other and needed ice-breaking *anesthetizers* to ease the social awkwardness of two heady and headstrong academics. But, I didn't want such dalliances to become a lifestyle. He didn't see the excessive drinking, eating and spending my money as a problem; for him, there was no problem! That is where we differed. I was coming to see that I couldn't relax around someone who seemed so clearly deceiving himself about how unhappy he was and trying to drown that misery with booze, food and spending money. Because I came from a family with similar addictive behaviors—they, too, lived in extremes as a rule and stuck their heads in the sand when it came time to facing their responsibilities—I was especially scared.

"Everything that irritates us about others can lead us to an understanding of ourselves."
—C.G. Jung

What Richard does or does not do with his emotional needs and bodily desires is up to him. It is his business, it's his karma—he will have to face his own choices. If he's going to dance, he'll have to pay his own piper! I cannot do anything to contain his voracious "dragon" as well as my own! My job is to tame my own "dragon" in a loving way and come from honest compassion. I've gathered this non-attachment practice from Twelve-Step friends and have within them felt the wisdom of the 9th century Chan master Linji who says, "If you understand, things are just as they are and if you do not understand, things are just as they are."

"So be not frightened if sadness rises up before you larger than any you have ever seen... Life has not forgotten you, it holds you in its hand; it will not let you fall. Why do you want to shut out of your life any agitation, any pain, any melancholy, since you really do not know what these states are working upon you... just remember that sickness is the means by which an organism frees itself of foreign matter. So you must be patient as a sick man and confident as a convalescent; for perhaps you are both. An more: you are the doctor too, who has to watch

over himself…and still there are many days when the doctor can do nothing but wait."
—*Rainer Maria Rilke*

Some days, walking feels more like negotiating a loosely-woven tightrope in rote, one-eye-opened prayer—other days, I think less and live more spontaneously, confidently in the unknown. A slogan of Al-Anon says, "Accept the present and tomorrow will take care of itself." Sometimes, accepting the present seems to be so much easier without Richard-the-addict in my sphere. I don't know. At other times, I'm overwhelmed with big waves of love that seem to come from beyond myself [ego?], and this love goes against my own rational standards of what is acceptable. As Swiss psychologist Carl G. Jung says, paraphrasing the Gospel of St. Thomas (70), "the darknesses we don't bring to light may kill us."

Using neurotic energy to be creative is the antidote for depression or suppressed-aggression, says Freud. Most of the Victorian "Hysterics" of the 19th century whom Freud analyzed were women-too-smart-for-their-times who were trying to be "well-behaved women," "good wives and mothers" or "appropriate ladies." Freud claimed such energy, if faced and integrated, could be the birth of creative insight. So many of us prefer the safe "womb" of our own misery—what Chogyam Trungpa Rinpoche calls "cocooning."

So many of us think of "falling apart" as our worst fear. We do everything in our power to create the appearance of having it all together. The neighbor lady I grew up next to—I'll call her Mrs. Stricklen—regularly washed the interior and exterior of the house every Saturday, including the garden hose! From the outside, everything shone brightly and seemed "squeaky clean." One afternoon, her college son strapped on a vest of dynamite and threatened to blow himself up in an attempt to get his old girlfriend to take him back. My guess is that he thought he was punishing her, (and everyone for whom he held a grudge), by detonating that dynamite.

Mrs. Stricklen, and the rest of the neighborhood remained speechless for what seemed to be months. She was unable to let herself go through what I consider to be a natural process of cracking open. This cracking open only turns into "cracking up" entirely if there's no coming together with sympathetic others who are willing to share in one's particular loss. Does the resistance to trauma through perfectionism enable a bigger fall or does it simply guarantee pain due to the solidified exterior?

I believe this "proper" middle-class, largely-White, Anglo-Saxon, Protestant (WASP) ideal punishes "the Stricklen's" of the world. Such perfectionistic standards are tragically brittle and hard to shed, but must be "come off" if any new growth is to follow. Perhaps Mrs. Stricklen had to fall apart in her isolated prison of perfection before she could reach out for the help she needed. Her hard stance against life only lengthened her fall and prolonged her suffering. Her polished, ice-sculpture-like exterior never gave her the promise of admiration or friendship for which she was waiting and striving. Letting people get to know her shame and anguish was the way she came back to life.

Life can only be felt as real if we share it with others. Isolating through perfect exteriors is like slamming the door; "Go away!" is the only message others can hear through our chilly façades. Paradoxically, we can only really "be together" when we have the deep capacity to fall apart and share ourselves with others. To "let people in," we have to accept our own limits and imperfections or there'll be no invitation to really get to know each other. As Albert Camus has said, "The bad news is: there is no salvation apart from one another. The good news is: we're all in this together."

But how can we fall apart gently, without losing our minds, jobs, and loved ones? I have found the best way to let the "ice" melt is through the heat of mindfulness meditation as well as through friendships found in trustworthy circles of support—like Twelve-Step groups. But, be assured, that "armor" will be coming off one way or another. It's like holding a helium balloon under water that is full of secrets. The more secrets stay hidden through isolation, the bigger the balloon and the tougher the struggle to conceal it. Explosion or implosion need not be our only choices if we can let those secrets rise to the surface and be shared.

"Life is being as it is."—*Joko Beck* author of *Nothing Special*

Making This Practice My Own (set timer for 10")
Close your eyes and pay attention your breath as it enters and then leaves your body. Once you are in a calm, balanced physical and emotional state, ask your Higher Self, "What is it that I desire now?" Gently allow your Higher Self (or what Quakers call "Inner Teacher") to answer this question. Do not block, judge, or censor the answer. Simply accept whatever comes. Continue

breathing easily for a few minutes. Make it your intention to focus on creating this dream. Then, when you are ready, or when the timer goes off, slowly open your eyes.

Set the timer for 20" and write about what your answer to the question: "What is it that I desire now?"

Losing Ground to Gain the Whole World

"I have held many things in my hands, and I have lost them all; but whatever I have placed in God's hands, that I still possess."
—Martin Luther

"Your proper concern is alone the action of duty, not the fruits of the action. Cast then away all desire and fear for the fruits, and perform your duty."—*The Bhagavad-Gita*

In the fall of 2001, while keeping my mind on the spiritual value of "taking action and letting go of the outcome," I went to meet a degree-granting colleague in the Psychology department of my University at the time. My aim was to discover how I could become an accredited or licensed professional psychologist. I had four degrees (one in psychology, one in theology, one in philosophy and the PhD in psychology and religion). I had five years of pastoral counseling training as a Chaplain with an accredited supervisor, and had years of support-group time, both as facilitator and as "participant-observer"—which is a veiled way of saying I was just another needy member of the group but wanted to keep the LOOK of an academic doing research. As my peers remind me, I had some good motives for being at therapeutic groups, too.

As I shook hands with the accreditation expert named Marc, he invited me to sit down in a chair that dwarfed me by about three feet. I propped myself up on pillows and leaned on the arm of the chair for symbolic parity. Eventually, I switched chairs so we could both look at the computer screen and see which requirements I had already met and which ones I had yet to acquire for accreditation. Throughout the entire 50 minutes of this informational interview I kept sinking into the chair as well as into self-doubt: "Should doing what we love to do feel this hard? Maybe I have always run away from tedious labor like this and maybe that's why I don't yet have this license. Perhaps it's my personality to avoid details, or maybe I'm sabotaging my professional independence. What am I afraid of?"

Because of my anxiety at the time, I kept focusing in-and-out of being able to concentrate on what Marc was actually saying. Afterward, he mentioned an alternative to the bureaucratic process of accruing four more years of post-graduate counseling hours and about 20 classes with psychology in the title: Family Psychology, Developmental Psychology, Psychological Statistics, Group Psychology, etc. I realized then that my secular psychological background came only during my undergraduate years. The three degrees after my psychology undergraduate degree all had the word "religion" folded into them. I felt defeated, fearing that I would only qualify for a "spiritual counselor" degree and that such a license would make it difficult to ever work with non-religious clients, especially in the South! So my dream to get licensed as a clinical psychologist started to fall apart right under my feet.

Marc offered me an alternative suggestion. He urged me to consider "coaching"—a new field opening up that happens over the phone or e-mail and is very goal-oriented. "It seems like it would be more appropriate for my temperament as well," I thought to myself. I wasn't sure how next to proceed. Then, Marc handed me a flyer for a workshop that was occurring the following weekend in Atlanta. I vocalized a little aspiration (prayer or wish) with my open palms that went like this: "I want to use my natural talents in rewarding ways; if this coaching path is a wise idea, may I have the energy, enthusiasm and follow-through to pursue this vocation until more is revealed?"

As I read more about Coaching, I became cautiously interested. I liked the idea of being an authoritative resource to people over the Internet or by telephone; so much of what I did *naturally* was to counsel people who solicited my advice. My collective phone bills often hit the $800 dollar mark. Perhaps coaching could be my second income. As I thought more about it, it seemed to be a natural fit for my set of skills. My sense is that any career advice I had given to others always included the following themes: "Access your skills not only by *what comes naturally* but by *what seems to energize you* when you do it. Then take one *next right action* in that direction and let go of the results." And here was my chance to do just that.

What was my *next right action*, you may wonder? I built my own webpage:

www.mylifedesignunlimited.com and then got online to design my logo for my business card and stationary. Within a week, four women friends and I decided to start up a networking support group for "creative consultants" who were working as independent contractors. As soon as I had those cards in hand, off I went to present myself to future clients. This was one gift of "the program" of Al-Anon which says, "keep the focus on yourself, for YOU are the only one you can change." As the book *The Dilemma of the Alcoholic Marriage* claims, "I will remind myself...that I am powerless over anyone else, that I can live no life but my own. Changing *myself* for the better is the only way I can find peace and serenity." One thing I have since learned is that to do this kind of changing, I need the support of loved ones or at least kind-hearted friends. As Reinhold Niebuhr has said, "Nothing we do, however virtuous, can be accomplished alone; therefore, we are saved by love."

I chose the title of this section, (*Losing Ground to Gain the Whole World*), because it often feels like we are sacrificing our most prized possessions when we put our dream out there as a wish or a goal and nothing seems to happen right away, if ever. What I find is that we cannot keep what we are not ready and willing to give away.

For example, in the Biblical story of Genesis, Yahweh asks Abram to go to Mount Moriah to make a sacrifice to him. Yahweh tells Abram to bring his most beloved son Isaac (Ishmael is the most beloved son sacrificed in the Islamic version of the same tale) to sacrifice, and he tells Abram to trust him. Abram doesn't even question Yahweh—even though, for all rational purposes, he could have. After all, Yahweh told Abram he would be made "the father of all nations and would have multiple offspring." This book says that Abram was almost 100 years old at the time of this promise and had only two sons: Isaac, born of Sarah and Ishmael, born of his midwife, Hagar. And now Yahweh asked Abram to "Prepare to give up Isaac to me as a sacrifice. Trust that I will provide." Against all parental instincts and the simple logic, Abram abides and, after traveling for three days with his son, stops to build an altar atop which he will lay his son Isaac as a sacrifice. Obediently, Abram raises up the knife used in this type of sacrificial ritual, and, just then, Yahweh brings him a ram to take the place of Isaac. All is well and many offspring arrive down the lineage of Abraham (formerly Abram) and Sarah (formerly Sarai)— Abraham, indeed, becomes the father of nations and this story is re-told by the three faiths of Islam, Christianity and Judaism.

I reiterate this oft-repeated tale because it reveals the quality of all intention-setting or wish-making. We are able to desire with all our hearts whatever we want. But, with the same fervor, we must be willing to let it go, trusting that whatever replaces it will also be good (or, as monotheists would say, "God's will"). This seems to be the only kind of sacrifice that guarantees we will "gain the whole world" as a result of letting go. As the I've since learned that all I had to do was become the least bit willing to open my clutched fist a tiny, grudging bit to experience miracles. The Japanese writer, Toyohiko Kagawa says, "God alone knows the secret plan of the things God will do for the world using my hand."

Abraham, of course, wanted Isaac alive, but had to enact in his heart a behavior of profound willingness to let that desire go. As a result, he received not only Isaac's life, but a multitude of offspring soon afterward (so the story goes). Many religious traditions claim that it is best to ask for what we want with an open hand, knowing that all things come and go like the weather—bounty or its absence is never personal.

"No one can think clearly when their fists are clenched."—*G.J. Nathan*

"Gaining the whole world" can only come when we are prepared to let go of self-serving desires that turn into ego-demands which always result in future misery. A friendly teacher of Hinduism that I know from India once said to me, "The creator wants to give you whatever your heart's desire is—your happiness is most secure, however, if your greatest desire is your creator."

Making This Practice My Own (set timer for 10" for walking meditation)
Keep your eyes "soft" and pay attention to your breath as it first enters and then leaves your body as you begin walking slowly. Focus your full attention on your Heart's Desire[6] and notice any mental distractions that come up in your thoughts. As you continue to breathe and focus on your dream, take a look at what pulls your

---

[6] For more exercises on heart's desire see Sonia Choquette's book, *Your Heart's Desire: Instructions for Creating the Life You Really Want* (New York: Three Rivers Press, 1997).

attention away. Look at these distractions in a nonjudgmental way and notice whether they are fears, worries, other people's opinions, or beliefs that you have outgrown. As you continue breathing and walking slowly, see these distractions as being pulled out of your consciousness by gravity and swallowed into the earth. Imagine your conscious and unconscious mind coming together to form a single focus, like a needle on a compass, pointing directly toward your dream. As you walk, imagine your body, mind, and spirit filling with grace and ease of being. As you end this meditation, make a conscious choice to be receptive to experiencing your dream with each breath you take from this moment forward. When you are ready, or when the timer goes off, slowly open your eyes.

There's No Place Like Home

"Foxes have holes, and birds of the air have nests; but the Son of Man has nowhere to lay his head."–*Matthew 8:20*

Since 1981, after graduating from high school and moving to Seattle, then New Jersey, Rhode Island, New York and Georgia, I considered myself *just like Jesus* when it came to the idea of *home*. Up until recently, whenever I've been asked, "Where's home for you, Jennifer?" I've answered, "I move around a lot...*just like Jesus*, I have no place to rest my head." But, unlike Jesus, I thought, I justified my patterns of manic-defensive living—never being able to stay in one place for too long or with any one person or group, because, *to belong* to anyone or any community might mean we would both uncover the ordinary truths of myself, i.e., that I was just as human, limited, insecure, fearful and confused as everyone else.

To stay still, for me, always meant to make myself vulnerable to the fault-finding, scrutiny of others. To be mobile meant that I was a moving target; I never had to be counted on in any way that could disappoint others. I could be like an angel or more fittingly, a Buddhist Bodhisattva of compassion—that impossible ideal with 10,000 generous arms, who shows up at the right time to help others reach enlightenment or put an end to their suffering, and poof, she's gone. "Her work is done here folks, nothing to see here but the traces of a good person. We'll remember her fondly…and only wonder a little why she never calls again or keeps in touch."

So that was my fantasy, born of both my Catholicism and special brand of Buddhism: "to bring joy" and "an end to sorrow for others" and to not stick around to see our special relationship fade into the predictably mundane. One year I moved seven times in the same state of Rhode Island. Was I being stalked, you may wonder? No, but close. I was addicted and, in turns, repulsed by my addiction to an addict. His name was Christian. What's important is that he too, (just like Jesus), had "no place to rest his head" and like lost puppies in a box, we periodically comforted and emotionally-tortured each other but could never really help each other move out of that particular box we were in. This box or rut was one that allowed us to distract ourselves from adult risk-taking, normalized self-pity and made sense of anesthetizing behaviors—his drinking and pot smoking, my dieting and periodic bingeing on popcorn, margaritas or transcendental meditation (TM).

When these compulsive distractions (addictive behaviors) stopped anesthetizing me—I'd move on temporarily. Eventually I got a job in Long Island, New York working at a Quaker College. This job pulled me into greater self-respect and professional demands to assist others in a steady and predictable way. This was my first sense of making my own home.

When I met Richard I was still "on the move" and so was he. He had the same insecurities about being known as I had—we both were always needing to impress or please people, never believing that connecting with them in a simple and relaxed way would suffice, never trusting that we were enough. Some Twelve-Steppers call this kind of anguish a "dis-ease" born of growing up in emotionally-troubled households. Oftentimes addicts and their loved-ones have difficulty being in one place for too long without tremendous anxiety—what AA founder Bill Wilson calls "anxious apartness." They come to believe that this uncomfortable feeling of uniqueness/separateness demands anesthetizing. Many times, their offspring have the same difficulty, but, instead of substance abuse, they will normally find other mental escapes (reading compulsively, watching TV, computer games, tuning out through daydreaming, obsessive-compulsive behavior of some kind, etc.).

Some of us, co-addicts, addictively take the emotional temperature of whomever we're around with an aim to please or impress them in order to feel worthy of their company. Others of us create emotional chaos for ourselves as our primary mode of self-distraction—all of this is shame and fear-driven; it is often motivated by fear of facing our feelings about our **life as it is**.

When Richard met me, he said, "I've found my twin soul." I now see that this observation was no compliment but rather a kind of *folie à deux*. In our mutual delusion, we both thought: "We can really hide out well with this excelling and exceptionally gifted person; we'll never have to be known very deeply, but we can still get the illusion of companionship. This will be a kind of *achieving* friendship." This was truly the *familiar*— the compulsive and intimacy-avoiding family we'd both known so well.

"The world cannot be discovered by a journey of miles…only by a spiritual journey…by which we arrive at the ground at our feet, and learn to be at home." *–Wendell Berry*

I now can see clearly that both Richard and I had a "love-hate"- relationship with the idea of "home." For both our homes-of-origin were mixed with spotty affection, lots of drive to be the best (achiever and philanthropist, depending on the gender), and all kinds of mind-numbing habits to reward workaholic-martyrdom: drinking to excess, spending, overeating, chronic-dieting, extreme isolating, exacting rules, emotional-disconnect and at least one "out of it" parent due to mental illness or addiction. Both Richard and I had no sense of a serene place on which to model our sense of home. I now see that we needed to cultivate "home" within ourselves and with others in our community rather than continue to seek it in busy-ness or in a physical place.

Making This Practice My Own (set timer for 10")
Sit or lie in a position that you can hold relatively still comfortably. Close your eyes if you like and take a couple of really deep breaths, feeling your breath going in and out and noticing your chest rising and falling. Now bring your attention to the top of your head and wish your head well. May my mind be clear and spacious like the sky, may all anxious thoughts and feelings drift away

like clouds. May my mind be filled with ease, well-being, and serenity. Imagine this feeling of well-being (as if it were heat) moving down your face—around your eyes, your nose, your cheeks, and moth so that all the muscles of your face begin to soften and relax. Imagine the warmth of well-being moving into your jaw, down your neck, across your shoulders, down your arms, and into your hands and fingers, so that the top part of your body feels light and easy. Let the relaxation flow down your back, vertebrae by vertebrae, washing away any tightness or icy tension. Let the relaxation radiate through your chest, around your heart, in your stomach so that all knots are untied and everything is soft and easy.

Let the well-being move through your hips, down your legs, into your feet and toes. Take a moment to enjoy all the warming muscles of your body working together in harmony, with no tightness and no tension. Take a couple of really deep breaths, being aware of your breath going in and out, feeling your chest rising and falling.

Now visualize yourself as you are now or at some other tender time in your life. Take the image of yourself, place it in your heart, and surround it with care and tenderness. When the timer rings, let yourself chant (say) this *Metta* or Buddhist loving-kindness aspiration:

May I be safe and protected.
May I be happy and peaceful.
May I be strong and healthy.
May I take care of myself with joy.

Pushing Life's River

"Separate reeds are weak and easily broken; but bound together they are strong and hard to tear apart."—The Hebrew *Midrash*

"Being an artist means, not reckoning and counting, but ripening like the tree which does not force its sap and stands confident in the storms of spring without the fear that after them may come no summer."—*Rainer Maria Rilke*

For years I thought determined will power could force my desired outcomes in life. For example, as a five-foot, seven-inch tall, medium-boned white teenager living in the late 1970s, I wanted to be size five when I was size 11. Instead of accepting my genetic heritage, I starved my way down to size seven and then ballooned up past the size of the largest-sized jeans I owned (13). Pretty soon, I realized that thinking about squeezing into any pair of jeans made me even more depressed and even more tempted to seek solace in food or weight-loss schemes (sometimes both simultaneously!).

I eventually started wearing those balloon-like stretchy pants that one sees on dancers and hip, Latino *low-riders* alike in the 1980s. For you *policia facionista*, not to worry, by age 17 it was the

1980s, so I was in fashion! Little did anyone know that I was hiding out behind those pants because I couldn't trust myself to feed myself on demand without needing to change pants sizes in the very same day to accommodate my compulsive-binge-starving behavior. It sounds absurd to the person who does not struggle with an eating disorder and body-image problem—but the rest of you know what I'm talking about.

In hindsight author Geneen Roth is right, "for every day of starving there is a day of binge-eating."[7] I see that much of my binge-starve dance was about lacking any kind of authentic trust in myself—in my instincts. I lacked belief that I would do for myself what was in my best interest. I did not have an internalized sense of a reliable caregiver or protector. Both my parents had irregular relationships to food and one of my parents was an alcoholic. In their anxiety about their addictions, they focused a great deal on

---

[7] Geneen Roth, *When Food is Love: Exploring the Relationship between Food and Intimacy* (New York, Plume Press, 1993).

keeping up appearances and struggled daily to "look *normal?*" They achieved normality for as long as they could, during the day, and then, like vampires at night, they would give into their hungers—binge-drinking for my stepfather and binge-eating for my mother. As a result, I had internalized these lessons by becoming a "people pleaser," "second-guesser" and an "appearance-up-keeper" myself. These are symptoms of white, middle-class femininity, I know, but I could not shake them no matter how many feminist tracts I read and even tried to write. I eventually joined a women's support group in 1982 and embarked upon the journey of learning the power of self-acceptance and self-trust. We needn't believe these values will work to put them into practice and witness them working. At times we try so hard that we fail to see that the light we are seeking is within us.[8]

"By yielding you may obtain victory."
—*Ovid*

---

[8] See Cheri Huber, *That Which You Are Seeking is Causing You to Seek* (Murphys: CA, Keep It Simple Books, 1999).

Making This Practice My Own:

Trust Exercise

"The illusion of freedom is that it is getting away from things you don't like. I believe that freedom is working with what is."
—*Jerilyn Munyon*

Whatever you're resisting today—in hopes that forcing it into hiding will make it go away—focus on that struggle right now. Where do you locate that struggle in your body? What does it feel like? What size is it? What name would you give it? Now ask that name—say, for instance, *stuck-in-doubt-man:* "*Stuck-in-doubt-man*, I breathe you into me and ask you to take up as much space as you need." Now take a deep, deep breath and let all the resistance and tension loosen up as you exhale. Feel the relief that comes from letting go of the struggle. Experiment with this. Breathe in *stuck-in-doubt-man* and breath out a trust in the flow of life on life's terms. Breathing in *Mr. Stuck*, breathing out trust in the flow of life's river. Whatever we think will be helped by forcing it to happen, we need to see as a river that does not benefit in any way from our pushing it. It flows on its own.

"Awareness is so much better for me than closing out all feelings, shutting out people, withdrawing from living. No matter how hard the truth is or what the facts are, I prefer to know, look at, and accept this day."
—Al-Anon's *As We Understood*

My Mind, My Cure

"If the doors of perception were cleansed, everything would appear to us as it is, infinite. For we have closed ourselves up, til we see all through the narrow chinks of our cavern."—
William Blake

"The intellect has little to do on the road to discovery."—*Albert Einstein*

There are some people who want to go straight to the experience of Nirvana—the great release from the cycle of suffering. Then there are those people, like me, who would prefer, first, to read a book on it!

Something within me has always wanted mental mastery over any kind of direct-experience or cultivation-born mastery. I used to see my *bibliophilia* (love of reading) as a boon; it meant that I was a rigorous scholar and studious person, not a slacker who surfs from this high wave to that high mountain-top experience in search of the next ecstatic sensation. In my life now, I see that need for mental mastery as *bibliotherapy*...it's fine for a little while but it can become an obstacle to my taking the next intuitive risks that an evolving life demands. Just reading about "making a meaningful life" is one way, among many, where I can hold myself back from being open to what's in front of me if I would only walk outside the cavern of my own mental making.

What has made any of us feel we need to have mental mastery over experiential wisdom? Who taught us to value the notion of "mind over matter" or that mind and body were not one? Where did we get the idea—something in most every religious tradition—that the bodily appetites were dangerous and out to trick us into shameful behavior that would only feel delectable for a second before we'd crumble, (like the New Testament's Paul and Augustine after him), into feelings of despair and lament, "I do not what I want, but I do the very thing I hate" [Romans 7:15].

Where do we get the notion that our bodies, and the sensual feelings that arise from them, can never be fully trusted? "The senses, more often than not, deceive us," as the father of the Enlightenment, René Descartes (1596-1650), warned us. Even Gautama Siddartha (563 – 460 BCE), the title given to the founder of Buddhism, is recorded to have warned his once-married disciple, Subhuti, to resist the wish to return to his wife by saying, "It would be better for a man to put his member into the mouth of a snake than for it to enter a woman." The early Church fathers often chastised the non-celibate believer. The third-century North African

Catholic named Tertullian of Carthage (160-240 CE) once said, "Castration is better than marriage, for women's bodies are the gateway to hell."

These clearly, anti-female and anti-sensual hierarchies of spirit, mind, and body are old ones begun long ago and woven into a variety of mythic tapestries that make up the clothing we modern people wear. Seeing some of the toxic threads of this dank cloak can help us begin the necessary work of freeing ourselves from its residual effects. Cultivating creative ways to tap into the wisdom of our bodies is another way to throw off some of the misogynistic heaviness. But most importantly, letting go of mastery-pursuits altogether might be a fine way to work with what is, just **as it is**. This might be the skill that is truly meaningful.

Making This Practice My Own:
Whenever you're next in a public restroom, bless the mirror before you leave by saying, "May all

who come here see their unique beauty and be healed from shame."

When you are on a crowded bus or subway or walking down the street, try sending loving thoughts to each person you see within a space of 10 minutes. Just look at each person, smile, and say silently, "You are perfect the way you are!" Notice any changes in your mood. A good time to practice this is while waiting in line at the post-office or the supermarket.

If you are involved in a confrontation and your adversary is very angry, try (silently—or you may get punched!) saying, "May you be happy" or "I wish you well." Does your adversary's stance soften? Do you still feel attacked?

If you use email or instant messaging (IM), send a *Metta* phrase to everyone in your address book. Do you feel embarrassed? Is it difficult for you to wish others well? How does it feel to just send the message anyway?

Try extending loving-kindness as far as you can—see how it boomerangs back to you ten-fold. Your heart is opening as you plant the seed (of loving kindness). Overtime, *Metta* blossoms to include everyone. We begin to realize that all beings deserve unconditional love, including ourselves. When we practice relating to ourselves with kindness, generosity and acceptance, we become much more happy to give this gift to others (*for fun and for free*—without strings attached).

Breathing Mindfulness

"If we are perfect and complete, exactly as we are, 'lacking nothing,' as the Buddha says, then why all this emphasis on mindfulness, storytelling and community? Mindfulness, storytelling, and community are where we realize our perfection."—*William Alexander*

"The miracle is not to walk on water. The miracle is to walk on the green earth in the present moment, to appreciate the peace and beauty that are available now."
—*Thich Nhat Hanh*

When I worry about not having enough money to make ends meet, I often try the technique of "putting it out of my mind" in the hope that the tidal wave of anxiety I feel will go away. After a few years in support group—just after losing my grandfather to a fatal stroke—I began the technique of *breathing in* the very thing I was afraid of—impoverishment—and, via exhaling, *releasing* the notion that "I have exactly what I need for now."

One day, on my 70-mile commute to work to the University, I "breathed in the fear" and "released the calm that I was seeking" for the entire ride to work. I found myself slipping into a warm "tub of peace" without escaping into fantasy or hyper-attending to my worst fears. Two weeks later, my grandmother died. I was so grateful to have discovered a practice that helped me grieve the loss of both grandparents and that I could work with for the stress-filled months that followed. It was a first for me to find non-destructive ways to soothe myself through difficult feelings— something I had never been able to do prior to that point in time.

Tibetan tradition that is called *Lojong* or *Tonglen* practice and I was first exposed to it through Tibetan teacher Pema Chodron, Trungpa Rinpoche's senior Dharma student, who is now head Abbess in Nova Scotia's Gampo Abbey. This breathing exercise includes "mindful" or "relaxed attention" given to the feelings that arise during meditation without getting overwhelmed by these emotional experiences.

This practice works nicely with what Anonymous program members refer to as "turning it over" or "working Step Three."[9] It's precisely through working with this feeling-filled, mindfulness practice—carried on the wings of my breath—that I have found the greatest comfort and relief. No need to rush out of uncomfortable feelings into anesthetizing with food, alcohol, spending, or hyper-fixating on the problems of others to find relief from an anxious mind. We can go into the feeling and witness its

[9] Step Three, from the Twelve Steps of Alcoholics Anonymous, "Made a decision to turn our will and our lives over to the care of God as we understood Him."

transience. The thing we are each searching for is already within each of us. No drug, perfect mate, or financial windfall can provide the calm we can create through nurturing it via our mindful breathing.

Breathing mindfully is like listening to waves on an ocean, always available to attend to—the ebb and the flow of our very own, breath-spirit (L. *spiritus*). This practice takes practice. It's like training a skittish, stray cat to "stay still" and trust that today will take care of itself. To begin this practice, experiment with focusing on what you are dreading right now and work with it in this exercise (below).

Making This Practice My Own:

The Practice of *Tonglen*

Each of us has a "soft spot": the place in our experience where we feel vulnerable and tender. This soft spot is inherent in appreciation and love, and it is equally inherent in pain. Often, when we feel that soft spot, it's quickly followed by a feeling of fear and an involuntary, habitual tendency to close down. This is the tendency of all living things: to avoid pain and cling to pleasure. In practice, however, covering up the soft spot means shutting down against our life experience. Then we tend to narrow down into a solid feeling of self-against-other.

One very powerful and effective way to work with tendency to push away pain and hold onto pleasure is the practice of *tonglen*. *Tonglen* is a Tibetan word that literally means "sending and taking." The practice originated in India and came to Tibet in the 11th century. In *tonglen* practice, when we see or feel suffering, we breathe in with the notion of completely feeling it, accepting it, and owning it. Then we breathe out, radiating compassion, lovingkindness, freshness; anything that encourages relaxation and openness.

In this practice, it's not uncommon to find yourself blocked, because you come face to face with your own fear, resistance, or whatever your personal stuckness happens to be at that moment. At that point, you can change the focus and do *tonglen* for yourself, and for millions of others just like you, at that very moment, who are feeling exactly the same misery. I particularly like to encourage *tonglen*, on the spot. For example, you're walking down the street and you see the pain of another human being. On-the-spot *tonglen* means that you just don't rush by; you actually breathe in with the wish that this person can be free of suffering, and send them out some kind of good heart or well-being. If seeing that other person's pain brings up fear or anger or confusion, which often happens, just start doing *tonglen* for yourself and all the other people who are stuck in the very same way. When you do *tonglen* on the spot, you simply breathe in and breathe out, taking in pain and sending out spaciousness and relief. When you do *tonglen* as a formal practice, it has four stages:

First, rest your mind briefly in a state of openness or stillness. Second, work with texture. Breathe in a feeling of hot, dark, and heavy, and breathe out a feeling of cool, bright, and light. Breathe in and radiate completely, through all the pores of your body, until it feels synchronized with your in-and out-breathe.

Third, work with any painful personal situation that is real to you. Traditionally, you begin by doing tonglen for someone you care about. However, if you are stuck, do the practice for your pain and simultaneously for all those just like you who feel that kind of suffering.

Finally, make the taking in and the sending out larger. Whether your doing tonglen for someone you love or for someone you see on television, do it for all the others in the same boat. You could even do tonglen for people you consider your enemies—those who have hurt you or others. Do tonglen for them, thinking of them as having the same confusion and stuckness as you find or yourself. This is to say that tonglen can extend indefinitely. As you do the practice, gradually, over time, your compassion naturally expands—and so does your realization that things are not as solid as you thought. As you do this practice, at your own pace, you'll be surprised to find yourself more and more able to be there for others, even in what seemed like impossible situations.[10]

---

[10] *Tonglen Exercise* by Tibetan Abbess Pema Chodron from *When Things Fall Apart: Heart Advice for Difficult Times*

Universality of "Surrender"

"Letting go, turning it over, and keeping it simple is difficult. Sometimes when I feel exceptionally stressed, surrender does not come easily. Ultimately I must even let go of the surrendering process."—Al-Anon's *Hope for Today*

I'm having trouble writing right now, some call this writer's block. I wonder if my writer's block has any connection to feeling this intimacy block in my marriage? Some people say that they have to try everything to control the changes they seek in relationships before they'll surrender to the Universe's wisdom. That's me! I'm struggling to "let go and let love evolve on life's terms." My friends ask me, "Why do you stay with a man (my husband) who is clearly your shadow?" I say, "He's like Linji, the crazy wisdom Chan/Zen master of the 9th century who forced his disciples again and again to return to their inner wisdom instead of looking to him to give them direction and praise."

What's odd is that Richard, unlike Linji, never offered wise counsel in any neutral way, like what the Buddha has said, for instance: "Be a light unto yourself." Rather, Richard often says, "I'm the *real* scholar in this relationship, I know best, listen to me and you'll be on the right track." And then he proceeds to try to force his own mantra of "I'm never enough" onto me.

One can **never** perform well enough, get buzzed long enough, or feel full enough, or paid (appreciated) well enough in his world—and the world he was raised within. Like many American's hell-bent on realizing the "American Dream," there's always a sense of "could- have-done or should-have done." Richard, just like the men in his family and mine continues to work himself to death in an effort to grab that illusive golden ring. He doesn't seem to be as paralyzed as I do by these increasingly high standards he holds for himself and others. My core-self won't let me keep up the deception that these goals are life-giving.

"It is the chiefest point of happiness when a person is willing to be who [s]he is."
—*Desiderius Erasmus*

When I compare myself to Richard, I find myself feeling inferior. I resent how self-conscious I am in relation to him. I, like so many women, have been taught to dismiss the strengths I might bring to friendship, to marriage. For instance, I am easier-going, I like to goof off, laugh loudly and jump on my neighbor's trampoline. I like to watch movie after movie, nap, go for walks, see friends, do "non-productive" stuff that doesn't build my resume—at least once in a while! I like to meditate, soak in a salt bath with just a dash or two of lavender oil, to be quiet, to get massages, get my feet and hands rubbed, cleaned and polished.

What does this have to do with surrender, you ask? Surrender is universal. Every religious tradition has the message to release human effort (or rational mind) for liberation—whether you call it salvation, redemption, or enlightenment.

The Daoist immortal Laozi supposedly encouraged his disciples in the skills of *Wu-Wei* (or unselfconscious action). The Hebrew prophet Ezekiel released *Ruach* (the spirit of life) by breathing over the dead bones of Israel's ever-increasing failed human efforts to keep their covenant (contract) with Yahweh; Buddha urged all to release the pursuit of the endless, changeless "I." The Sufi master poet, Rumi and Christian mystic, Meister Eckhart both sought union and prayed for release from the effort-filled, egoic self. Eckhart prayed, "Please protect me from the God I seek." He knew that he sought certainty and wanted to find God where God could not be found, reified (made solid), or defined by the believer who needed material evidence. All religions demand that the practitioner "let go." What is it going to take, a bruised forehead, a tragedy, some humiliating experience or fundamental, existential exhaustion? Whatever it takes, just let it take!

Islam—Arabic for "submit"—is derived from the root word *"salaam,"* which means "peace." My Muslim friend, named Mo, says, "When our individual and collective lives are in harmony with nature and with the will of the Creator, peace is inevitable." For many years in the 1980s, I was working as a battered women's counselor, and, as a consequence, I had seen too much abuse happen to women and people of color due to the conviction that they needed to "submit or die." As a result, "submission" had been a word that I had refused to fold into my spiritual lexicon. However, surrender seems more of a winning move when I think about it now.

I get all stifled, choked, tired, and exhausted when I fight the current of my life, its purposes, my limits, bodily set point, necessary boundaries in my marriage or my honest hunger for connection. Fighting against my instincts is the opposite of surrender. Resisting is the opposite of letting go. When I catch myself doing this particular dance of fighting that which feels like a whirlpool of reality, I notice that if I let go of resisting, if I can let the riptide carry me down into my feeling world, then, *voila*, it inevitably spits me back out into calmer waters which permits me to swim back to the shore refreshed instead of exhausted. I'm often surprised to see how much energy I actual have *after* surrendering my efforts to produce idealized outcomes in my life. When I accept rather, than buck, what's in front of me, I can act decisively and yet with a loose grip.

At age 14, I witnessed my alcoholic stepfather get caught in a riptide on the stormy shores of Maui. He had joined me in body-surfing during a thunderstorm. We were the only two people crazy enough to do this on that particular beach. He went way out there to show off and got caught in a vicious riptide. Because he fought and fought it, he almost drowned. When a life guard (who just happened to be jogging by) was able to retrieve him, his chest was swollen with deep shades of indigo blood from all his adrenalin. His own panicky efforts to fight the tidal pull almost killed him—he had to be forced to release his grip on his version of what was right and true at the time.

How like him we can become? When we get fixated upon a version of reality that we simply must change in that instant or we'll die, (at least it feels that way), we can actually make fatal mistakes due to our fixedness. To surrender our picture of reality, (some call this fantasy), for the gift of seeing life as it is—we can actually feel the shift. This shift is only brought about through loosening our grip.

Making This Practice My Own: (set timer for 10")
Choose a path for walking that's about 20 feet long (preferably outside, weather permitting). In

73

this meditation the object of attention will be the movement of your feet and legs, rather than the breath. Hold your hands in a position that's comfortable for you—hanging your hands loosely at your sides, clasped in front of your waist or behind your back, or in your pockets. It may be helpful to take short strides than you normally would. Keep your eyes open. Walk back and forth a few times at a normal pace, noticing each time a foot touches the ground. You may want to silently say, "touching," or "stepping." After some time, begin to slow your pace, noticing how your weight shifts from side to side as you step. If your hands are by your sides, you may become aware that they are moving, too. Notice how pleasant it feels to be moving naturally, without trying to get anywhere. After a little while, slow your pace still further and place the attention on each movement needed to take a step. Be aware of lifting the heel, moving the foot forward, and placing the foot on the floor. Carefully pay attention to each step. You may want to silently note "lifting," "moving," "placing" with each motion. If your mind wanders, stop; take a couple of deep breaths, feeling your breath going in and out; and then continue walking. There is no final destination—it's the process that's important. We are already there.[11]

We Talk Therefore We Are

"Despite the sometimes-overwhelming sense of mortification, I kept coming back to Al-Anon. In time I understood that though I wasn't alone in my suffering, I would continue to feel isolated as long as I chose to remain silent. So I began to open up and trust people. I started sharing my 'worst' secrets with the group. To my relief, telling my experiences was met with love and compassion."—Al-Anon's, *Hope for Today*

When I spoke to a friend of mine named Judith about my emotional loneliness and disappointment within my new marriage, she said, "Girlfriend, men don't talk—*we[women] talk, therefore we are!*" She went onto say, "For most

---

[11] Madeline Ko-I Bastis, *Peaceful Dwelling: Meditations for Healing and Living* (Boston: Tuttle Publishing, 2000).

75

men socially-conditioned to *be men,* it's like this: *We win, therefore we are!*" It is a lonely world for men who feel invisible unless they're triumphing over something or trumping someone. Aggressive positioning and competitiveness have been the ways most men have been raised to "relate" to earn from other males the most basic self-respect. With more and more people seeing the empty and lonely result of a competition-consumption existence, they are turning to spiritualities that value cooperation, intimacy and sharing of self with others.

The Twelve-Steps of A.A. have become touchstones for more than just the addict who wants to stay sober. There are spin-off anonymous programs with everything from over- (or under-) eating, to "debting," to gambling, to sex and romance addiction. Today, there are more places than ever to find people with whom you can talk and, thus, break out of your isolating shame. Talking, for both men and women, seems to help us break the alienation that fuels the cycle of addictions and self-destructiveness. Many have felt all "talked out," however, and wonder what comes after talk-therapies (one-on-one or in groups)? Many wonder, "How can I be alone without being lonely?" or "How can I know that I'm at peace or feeling okay without confirming it with others by talking all the time?" Such people are good candidates for meditation—where we begin to listen to the silence beyond our neuroses. By asking "who is this I?" in our meditation, we dismantle the idea that we have a permanent or rigid self that we've convinced ourselves *is* us. We can open up to the fluidity of wider perspectives born in silence.

"One of the illusions shared by many of us who have been effected by alcoholism is that only another person, usually the alcoholic, can fill that empty place within us. If only he were more attentive, if only she got sober, if only they were with me now, I wouldn't be lonely. But many of us remain just as lonely even after those conditions are met."
—Al-Anon's *The Courage to Change*

Meditation is a chance to get quiet with the fluid self of what Buddhists call our "original nature." It is time to reunite Atman (soul) with Brahman (the Universe)—from which all life comes, so say the Hindus. It is the time to "surrender to the God that is farthest away from what I could ever articulate," said Meister Eckhart. "Silence is golden," as the Pre-Socratic philosopher Epictetus said. Can we let go into the golden silence of not knowing, in any fixed way, who we are, not knowing what to prioritize? Can we sink into the quiet of "Great Mystery" as some Native Americans call it? What have we got to lose but the age-old narratives we fixate upon in our effort to possess a solid self or secure identity? Can we let the storyline go—even for 10 or 20 minutes? Can we just breathe in what Korean Zen master Seung Sahn calls, "Only don't know mind"?

"Today I will spend some time exploring the most intimate human relationship I will ever have—my relationship with myself."
—Al-Anon's *The Courage to Change*

"What a lovely surprise to discover how un-lonely being alone can be."—*Ellen Burstyn*

Making This Practice My Own: (set timer for 10")

Find a comfortable, quiet place to lie down, and gently close your eyes. Now take three slow; deep breaths allowing yourself to settle down and connect with whatever is supporting you right now. With each breath you exhale, allow yourself to feel the firm ground beneath you. Continue to focus on your breathing until you are in a quiet, balanced state. Now imaging gazing into a gentle blue sky. Imagine yourself dreaming, drifting, relaxed and peaceful as you gaze at clouds floating by. As you allow yourself to mentally drift, imagine a radiant light pouring down upon you, covering your body and warming you. Feeling relaxed and at ease, allow yourself to release tension with each breath you exhale. Squinching or tightening your entire body (even your lips) with the inhale and shaking it loose with every exhale. Do this a few times until you feel even more relaxed. Now, allow yourself to just breath normally, relaxing with each breath you exhale. Feeling safe, allow yourself to imagine the heat in your body as the force of life (love) in the universe. Let this force fill your entire being. Let your attention gently slip away from your thoughts and follow the warmth that resonates deep within you. Relax. Breathe. Listen. This is the ground of your being. This calm is available to you to be a source of guidance at any time. You can ask the force of life/love to remind you that you are always accompanied by this warmth, this calm, if you are willing to make time to cultivate it. When the timer rings, slowly open your eyes with gratitude.

No Saint Has Ever Made Me Laugh

When I told my longtime gal-pal, Whitney, that I was writing this chapter, she said she loved the title. I have this idea that it was precisely because a Bodhisattva (a Buddhist "saint" who forgoes her/his own enlightenment until all beings are free) lacked a sense of humor that the one he was trying to assist couldn't receive the gift of enlightenment. It's like Thoreau, the great American author and recluse, who said, "If I knew that a person was coming over to my house with the intention of saving me, I'd run like hell as far away as possible." No one wants *the Way* to be forced down their throat.

My sense is that enlightenment is an inner arrival of peace with whatever needs to be faced in this moment. A sense of calm and even a chuckle might wash over a person who is genuinely enlightened whether it's raining hail stones or not. Of course there are only enlightened *ways of seeing* not enlightened *states of being*. The Buddha knew this when he looked at a flower and smiled as he caught the insight of its simplicity in the eye of his disciple, Subhuti, who joined him in loving the entirety of that perfect moment. "To me," Walt Whitman once wrote, "every hour of the day and night is an unspeakably perfect miracle." Can I truly believe that in my heart?

When I speak of *genuine* enlightenment, I speak redundantly. I suppose there is no false enlightenment. This way of being cannot be faked though it can be cultivated, say the Chan masters of Buddhism in China. There is an age old debate between those who would hold that the enlightened journey is a gradual journey, a *Way* to be cultivated in living and seeing and those who would hold that enlightenment can happen in an instant and everything is seen from a wholly-transformed perspective forevermore. *Loving Life as It Is* comes from the gradual school of Buddhism but does not argue with the instantaneous school: To each her own way—no dogma necessary. It is fine if our path transforms our narrow vision into a wider focus of experience. But, enough about Buddhist philosophical debates; there are as many of those as there are schools of Buddhism.

"What does *Enlightened seeing* and *living* feel like? How do I know when I'm in it? How do I know

I'm doing it right?" my students of Buddhism ask me. What I might say, depending on the day, is that "only you know and you never really know in a verbal or rationally expressible way." At least that is what most Zen practitioners say to their disciples. Living is the test. The prophets of the Hebrew Scriptures were regarded as "the real deal" only when their predictions proved to be accurate. If they were wrong in their prophecies, they were imprisoned or executed by the King. In the Zen Buddhist tradition, Zen master Linji would use a stick on whoever doubted his or her own authentic nature, his or her own automatic, intuitive response. There's no faking enlightened seeing. It is the kind of seeing and being with all that is, **as it is**, that only the truly-centered can accomplish.

Students lament, "Well, does that leave behind those of us who cannot become dedicated monks who meditate all day in a monastery?" No, not if such practices would not help 21st century people living in modern cultures. Today we need tools and techniques that help us cultivate enlightened seeing right where we are in these particular times, places, relationships and bodies. We need help sinking into deeper awareness right now, when we change our baby's diapers, when we drive in traffic, when we can't sleep at night due to mentally obsessive storms, when we're really annoyed with a co-worker or housemate, when relatives come to visit, when we've just experienced a failure, loss, or a promotion of some kind.

All these are only a few examples of challenges that demand our cultivation of skillful seeing and living, one breath at a time. As we do this, we begin to face life as it is with greater ease of being. We can face life on life's terms without flipping out when people, places or things don't seem perfect, or don't seem to be going **our** way. We will come to see that life is neither *for* us nor *against* us. As it says many times in Hebrew Wisdom literature, "It rains on the poor and rich alike." Obstacles to you are not personal, and you needn't jump out the nearest window; you can face it with great ease born of acceptance.

Some of us grew up with a Santa Clause version of a deity who came around once a year to reward the good with goodies and punish the bad with a lump or coal or by withholding any reward. Letting go of this version of reality can be very difficult for most of us, but especially the majority of North Americans, raised in either the Jewish or Christian households. So many have been raised to believe in a God who rewards the dutiful and punishes the slacker. "If no one's up there measuring our actions, why should we do anything right?" asks one of my students in my Philosophy of Religion class. This was precisely Nietzsche's prediction, and I paraphrase him: 'If we believe in a God that judges good and evil, fear of punishment will become our only motivation for our actions, thus producing a learned doubt in our own capacity for anything good as humans.' Nietzsche called this tendency to please a wrathful god by stifling our instincts to thrive a kind of "slave morality." Sartre calls this "bad faith." "This is the God that must die for humans to evolve," says Nietzsche. I think he's right.

When I was 10 years old, I wanted to be a priest and go down in history as the first female Catholic who was so saintly that the Church opened its doors to allow women to be ordained—after all, who would want to lose out on all that goodness? When I was fourteen, I was told, "girls can't be priests." And I thought to myself, "That's weird! Then how can they be saints?" I found out later that no matter how good a female may be, no matter what she offers the world in terms of brilliance, generous service or humanitarian teachings through-action, she'll never be allowed to be a Roman Catholic priest—only men are permitted to be priests. No matter that many men in seminary are just as unbecoming in their conduct as those in the worst fraternities, as long as they are men, they can be priests.

In the late 1980s, our old seminary saying at Princeton went like this, "If you can **pee** like Jesus, you can **be** like Jesus!" or "No apostolic succession for the ladies," say the last centuries of popes and their minions. Yet, we women are permitted to still be saints and compete with other female-priest-"wanna-be's" for who can perform the greatest miracles of self-sacrifice.

Seven years after leaving the Catholic Church at age 21, I found myself meditating in a Japanese-style *zendo* wondering to myself, "Exactly what are you trying to accomplish, Jennifer?" The silent answer I gave myself was this: "I want to be good without God or an external measurer of goodness as my guide."

What I found later is that even the "godless religions"—as they're called here in the South—are ripe for inviting martyrdom, especially for the female adherent. In the first century school of Mahayana Buddhism, one had (and still has) the Goddess of compassion as the ideal of Buddhist love in the world. In China, she is called Kuanyin and is based on the tale of a princess Mioshan who is banished from the royal palace because she refuses to marry as her father had mandated. Because she disobeys his orders, he tries to kill her three times and even burns down the Buddhist convent where she lives with other women who chose the spiritual path of celibacy over marriage. As fate would have it, Princess Mioshan is spared each time. She eventually goes into hiding and takes on the attire of a male monk to protect herself from her father's intent to kill her for disobeying his will. As karma would have it, her father grows ill of a strange disease that only a potion made up of a pure being's eyes and limbs will cure.

Princess Mioshan finds out that her father is in search of such a pure soul and secretly gives his steward both of her arms and eyes to pulverize into a salve for the father's cure. The potion works, and, after being restored to health, the King and Queen want to reward the holy "man" who gave so unselfishly of himself. The steward leads them back to his daughter who, though still dressed like a monk, is recognized by the Queen and embraced. The King falls to his knees and prays that Lord Buddha would restore the limbs and eyes of his perfect daughter. Instantly, Princess Mioshan is rewarded for her bodily sacrifice and self-less love by becoming a Bodhisattva. Temples in China are dedicated to her much like churches are dedicated to "The Blessed Virgin Mary" or "Our Lady" in Roman Catholic Churches. It is important to remember that women can be just as neurotically self-sacrificing and self-mutilating in Buddhist traditions as in Catholic ones—especially if one is raised to be a "good girl" and dutiful, father's-daughter at all costs.

My new criteria for any ideal or any spiritual mentor is, "does she make me laugh?" Because, let's face it, balanced perspective, not self-abnegation makes the world so much more livable. I need a sense of humor, not a mission to save the world or earn my priestly/goddess-y stripes. Self-forgetfulness enables laughter and laughter helps us forget ourselves—it's a necessary cycle. Laughter is about loosening our grip in all things, but especially in relation to ego-identity positioning. There is a Buddhist story about a Bodhisattva who lost helping a person become enlightened precisely because she couldn't laugh at herself—or didn't get a joke.

Making this Practice My Own:

If I were to be decadent for one whole week what would I do?

Here are a few suggestions:

- Sleep in.
- Let other people pay this time.
- Stay up late.
- Drink tap water instead of bottle water.
- Make strangers laugh.
- Go skinny dipping.
- Don't call anyone you feel obliged to call.
- Dine in your pajamas.
- Say no to 10 people.
- Send yourself an arousing telegram/email.
- Take a "sick" day for your mental health.

- Say, "Let me think about it," to someone pressing you for an answer.
- Order "take out" or room service to be delivered.
- Eat with a lit candle with every meal.
- Hire a cleaning crew to clean the whole apartment/condo/house, even windows.
- Get a massage therapist to come to your house.
- Tell your roommate/partner that you're not lifting a finger this week.
- Give up counting calories/carbohydrates/fat grams forever (say to yourself, "scales are for fish").
- Ask for what you really want.

Alchemical Artwork

"If you bring forth what is within you, what you bring forth will save you. If you do not bring forth what is within you, what you do not bring forth will destroy you."—*The Gnostic Gospel of Thomas*

"We do not become enlightened by imagining figures of light, but by making the darkness conscious."—*C.G. Jung*[12]

---

[12] C.G. Jung, *Memories, Dreams, Reflections* trans. Aniela Jaffe (New York: Vintage Press, 1989).

The chemists of the Middle Ages used to believe they could find a potion that would transform iron into gold and discover the elixir of perpetual youth—this was the field of alchemy and these scientists were called alchemists. In Tibet, many Lamas of old believed they too could transform what first appeared worthless into a priceless asset. Pema Chodron has called this Ancient Tibetan practice *Tonglen*. As we've explored above, this meditation takes whatever feelings are unwanted and considered bad or worthless and works with them until they are transformed into the very peace we seek. We stop pushing away feelings with our habits of aversion and instead we invite them to be felt even more fully by breathing them in.

Many of us have intense feelings of depression, lack (material or emotional), or professional or intellectual inadequacy. We desperately try to run from these feelings, hoping they won't ever catch up to us, if we'd only run fast enough. We may try to stay extremely busy to avoid those feelings or keep ourselves striving and striving for even more professional successes, because that last success only gave us a short rush of pride, and the rushes for success seem to dissipate with ever-increasing speed. This *transitoriness* of confidence causes even greater anxiety, as if the truth of our lack (or hole in the center of our soul) will get bigger and bigger and eventually will swallow us whole. Pema Chodron invites those who feel this way to experiment with *Tonglen* meditation. This is the ultimate alchemical move. Breathe in the great lack that you feel and that countless others suffer from the welfare to workfare mom, to the recently-fired executive. Exhale the satisfaction and contentment that we all seek. Release it out of every pore of your being until such calm and peace is flooding yourself and those imagined others. The Buddha taught this technique (called *Maitri* in Sanskrit) that the Mahayana Buddhists believe is primary: That all beings be free from their suffering and the roots of suffering and that my own suffering will never be vanquished until all beings' sufferings are vanquished. This gives us great incentive to work not only on our own peace of mind, but peace in all our relations—peace in the world.

Making This Practice My Own: (set timer for 10")
Find a few pillows to prop yourself up with in bed. Make sure you feel your spine is fairly straight and supported. Gently close your eyes. With every in breath say, the first part of the *Maitri* Meditation (i.e., "May all beings be"), with every out breath say the second half, (i.e., "free from suffering and the roots of suffering").

Breathing in:
May all beings be free from suffering and the roots of suffering

Breathing Out
May all beings be free from ignorance and the roots of ignorance

Breathing In
May all beings be free from greed and the roots of greed

Breathing Out
May all beings be free from hatred and the roots of hatred

Breathing In
May all beings be free for joy and the roots of joy

Breathing Out
May all beings be free for wisdom and the roots of wisdom

Breathing In
May all beings be free for generosity and the roots of generosity

Breathing Out
May all beings be free for peace and the roots of peace

When the timer goes off, bring hands together in a prayer position and bow gently and slowly (to the basic goodness in you and in all beings) then open your eyes.

Finding a Seven-Year-Old Friend

"I am the breeze that nurtures all things green…
I am the rain coming from the dew that causes
the grasses to laugh with the joy of life."
—*Hildegard of Bingen*

"Imagination   is   more   important   than
knowledge."—*Albert Einstein*

For people who feel they are too busy to play,
too needed by others to ever sit down and relax,
or too important to be silly, they might be
helped, (as I was), by making friends with a
seven-year-old. The world of a seven year old is
often far more full of wonder about curiosity
that life presents than most people who claim to
have no time to pause and wonder. A seven-year
old can play at the drop of a hat by turning such
a hat into a prop that she uses in her nightclub
improvisation. My seven-year old friend's name
is Liza or Lisa (depending on her mood), and she
adores all manner of performing. She sings into
her make believe "mic" and prances around the
room in her vaudeville regalia. She lives to tell a
story   through   dance.   Other   times   she

communicates with unseen (to me, at least) fairies and invisible animal friends. She dresses up her cat "Zina" to accompany her routines and magic acts. Liza, like me (and many other girls and some boys) at her age, adore torch singers but especially loves lip-synching to Liza Minelli's greatest hits. She's a bundle of fire and endlessly self-entertaining through narcissistic self-celebration. I wonder what allows her to let so much energy find so many outlets. What makes other adults (like me) try to tamp down that multitudinous energy into one singular vocation that we call a career? This is the source of much repression, tension and stress. We've lost much of our passion to dance and sing, we adults.

Spontaneity in all its forms is a great pleasure and is a grave mistake to neglect. Like the art of writing, creative energy must come out and will do so no matter what—either directly or indirectly. Young people, like Liza/Lisa, don't fight this flow. We adults have so much to learn from them that making a seven-year-old friend is a great way to rekindle our friendship with our own inner seven-year olds and re-activate our heretofore abandoned innocence.[13]

Making This Practice My Own: (you'll need glue, scissors, and a poster board or cardboard box for this practice)

Be willing to "baby" sit for a friend (who has a child under age 12 and over age 6) this week in exchange for all the used magazines she or he has in the house and office. With the child or children you are watching, ask them if they can help you make a dream collage. Take any cardboard box or poster board and lay it on the ground between you and the child. Ask the child to help you cut out images and glue them onto the dream board. Together, you hope to make a

---

[13] As I write this, Cardinal Law is being expelled in the Catholic Church for shuttling one too many untreated pedophilic priests from parish to parish. I am aware that not all of us can "make friends" so innocently with a seven year old child. It is precisely because we adults are so alienated from our own child-likeness and erotic curiosity that this energy implodes and emerges in twisted and violent ways. More now than ever, we need to reclaim this energy rather than let it fester inside and ooze out sideways.

dreamy village or dreamy work of art with whatever colors, images, or words that catches their fancy in these magazines. Urge them (and yourself) to let imaginations run wild. They can use felt pens too, to write their own messages. Get them to help you push past your limited thinking. This can be very illuminating.

Breathing Space

"Our only enemies are guilt, fear and shame. Such unresolved negatives prevent us from living fully...."—*Elisabeth Kübler-Ross*

Lately, I've come to the insight that our spiritual practices, if we have them at all, can reflect our healthy habits or neurotic habits. What interrupts this conundrum? A good teacher with lots of learning experiences to draw from can be a good beginning. What makes me so sure our meditation or prayerful practices will reflect the same mistakes of thinking of our habitual approach to life, if untutored? Well, it's come up a great deal in recent conversation that I've had with other meditators. We've found that if we are tightly wound and a bit obsessive in our need to control ourselves and others, then we'll be drawn to very structured prayer or meditation rituals. We will move toward breath counting with a visible timer that rings its bell exactly at 20 minutes. Or we will need a formula of some kind like the rosary or a *mala* to count how many prayers (or chants) we've said in a row and perfectly!

If we're a bit too relaxed about the whole thing, even loose about whether we have had time today for prayer or meditation, we'll be the kind of meditator who, like Jack Kerouac's *Dharma Bums*, loves "Big Sky Mind," and "just being with the breath, moment to moment" or we'll prefer lying-down meditation to sitting upright. We'll be happy to see the sacred all around us—"no need for rituals or formulas of any kind, it's all within and all around us." These are examples of temperaments that could be helped by a teacher or guide. Teachers help each of us not to fall forward into our particular rigidities or to fall backward into our slackerly habits. Teachers can help bring our attention to work with our tendencies (or our "edge) and foster greater focus through awareness cultivation.

Breathing space is a way to discover your particular temperament. Creating a room where you can get into a kind of silent, undisturbed, meditation sitting position is vital to uncovering your own particular habits of being. Because how we breathe in "a room of our own" making is very much a mirror for how we live. People have said to me, "But there's no room at my apartment" or "I share a cell with an inmate; how can I meditate?" I've heard a lot of obstacles in my years as a scholar, educator and chaplain. I say, "If you can sit up with your spine straight, chin a little tucked in, tongue resting at the back of your front teeth, mouth slightly open, breathing in and out through your nose, you can meditate." Monks around the world (from all religious traditions that have monks) are challenged by street sounds, bunk-to-bunk crowding in their monasteries, jack hammers outside, etc. All of this is fodder for "turning it all over" and breathing deeply as we let go of needing everything to be comfortable or preferable. As Laozi, the Daoist immortal, was known for saying, "Need little, want less." Contentment is never far off.

Making This Practice My Own:

Make a list of 10 persons for whom I am grateful and why (in brief):
1.
2.
3.
4.
5.
6.
7.
8.
9.
10.

Make a list of 10 things that I am grateful for and why.
1.
2.
3.
4.
5.

6.
7.
8.
9.
10.

Make a list of 10 things that I could donate to charity? (If you have trouble doing this, try pulling out everything in your closets and put back only the things that you have used/warn over the past 365 days).

1.
2.
3.
4.
5.
6.
7.
8.
9.
10.

Now call a friend and ask her/him to do this same exercise. Make a commitment to meet at the local Salvation Army or nearby homeless shelter to share this wealth.

Making Time When None Can Be Found

"The unexamined life is not worth living."
—*Socrates*

"We need patience. Some wounds cannot be healed quickly. They must be given time. In the meantime, we can appreciate the new capabilities we are developing, such as the capacity to mourn and the willingness to accept. Let us share our losses and triumphs with each other, for that is how we gather courage."
—Al-Anon's *The Courage to Change*

"Today, like every other day, I wake up empty and frightened. Don't go to the door of the study and read a book. Instead take down the dulcimer, let the beauty of what you love be what you do. There are a thousand ways to kneel and kiss the ground, there are a thousand ways to go home again."—*Rumi*

Little by little, I realize that nobody ever *finds* time—it's not lost. Time is something that we manufacture for ourselves. Time is something that we carve out of the rocky schedule or impenetrable wall of activity in which we live. I'm coming to accept that time must be attended to, like a garden, or one will surely pay via its drying up; neglect produces parchedness. Time must be nurtured, it must be coddled and affirmed—doing so will ensure it will give back ten-fold.

So many Americans live lives that are frantically busy, driven by sense of lack, and without reflection. Socrates would roll over in his grave with our general lack of rigorous self-examination. "There's no time," we all snap back. "Who has time to examine their choices, their habits, their ways of being with others, their ways of being alone?" Do we ever think about what our busy-ness gives or promises us? Can we afford to live such unexamined lives? What would Socrates say? Is this lifestyle of frantic activity really worth living? "Time is money," they say. The truth is, time is what we make it to be. It's like an ordinary fabric—we can make with it a mat to rest upon or a noose to hang ourselves with…it's up to us.

At this particular time in my life, I'm making time to write—"just three pages a day," *Artist's Way* author Julia Cameron suggests. She calls them "morning pages" because they can start the flow of creativity the first thing in the morning, just like meditation. I call them "mourning pages" because, more often than not, they turn into a kind of lamentation of my half-lived life. Usually, they unearth the shadowy parts of myself that often experience sadness, fear or loss of some kind. If you were willing to take responsibility for making time for your reflection, what would you discover? Such unexpressed feeling often turns into depression or general moodiness. Everyone benefits when I use my "mourning pages."

Making This Practice My Own:
I commit to writing three pages a day this week, right after I get up in the morning.

I commit to move my pen on paper—without criticism for what I see during this time. I will not edit my words or thoughts, I will let my imagination run wild with thick description for what I'm feeling, seeing, noticing this moment.

During this time, I will let my brain drain out onto the page. I will let myself "let it rip" if I want to complain. I will let myself rant if I want to rant. I will let myself be full of self-pity if I want to be full of self-pity—accounting for all the wrongs done to me in my lifetime. If I want to moan, I'll moan while I do this. If I want to imagine myself in a horror movie, I'll spell out the details in my morning writing. If I want to imagine myself in some tawdry affair, I'll not miss a drop of saucy description. If I want to make this one long wish list, for seven whole days, that's just great. How does not holding back feel? Can you bring more of your plucky self (your "original nature") to what you do in work and love?

Walking *The Way*

"She who is centered in the Way can go where she wishes without danger. She perceives the universal harmony even amid great pain, because she has found peace in her heart."—*Dao De Jing*

"The Dao never does anything, yet through it all things are done."—*Laozi*

In the *Dao De Jing*, Laozi says, "The *Dao* that can be 'named' is not the eternal *Dao*." Following the *Dao De Jing*, Confucius says, "The *Dao* is discovered by walking it." There is no blueprint for walking *the Way*; it is like being a tightrope walker in a dense fog, it cannot be walked any other way. There is no getting in front of the rope. There is no contract guaranteeing that you, in fact, are on the *right* rope and are walking the correct way. Walking is making *the Way*—it's done as we go along with great attention to cultivating the self, for which Confucius meant harmonizing with our surroundings—with nature, with our relations—with things as they *really are* rather than with things as we wish they would be.

The Way or "*Dao*" in Chinese is not a thing or a fact to be "gotten right." Hence, no wars have been fought in the name of *the Way*. Daoism understands perspective as something that is infinitely plural or multiple. "Being with what is in all its variety is *the Way*." "The 10,000 things," or what Buddhists call "10,000 sorrows and joys," is another way of saying the same thing and is a phrase frequently used to point to multiple ways of seeing. Opening up to multiple ways of seeing is cultivating the self-in-relation to others, always in relation to the 10,000 things.

Today, I am walking this path as I go along. In the summer of 2001, I got married to Richard (my second marriage), a man I imagined as my soulful mate. We both loved meditation, traveling, reading and going to dinner with friends who shared our love for philosophy, movies and deep, red wine. Three months into the marriage, I wondered to myself, "How could I have mistaken this infant with someone with whom I could spend the rest of my life?" I say this because he was always sucking something dry, whether it was a bottle, his academic audience or me. I eventually came to see that I was living with this man as my affectionate roommate not as the soul mate for which I had longed. I kept feeling like there was a price to pay for any gift he gave me; nothing seemed to be given from a place of generosity, what Twelve-Steppers call "for fun and for free." Al-Anon taught me to use this slogan as a motto for all forms giving.

"I felt some regret along with these spiritual awakenings, but Al-Anon kept me busy learning about alcoholism as a disease…I wondered why I should try to fight alcoholism, so I decided to admit that alcoholism is more powerful than I. Now I am free to discover the person inside me who is spirited, fun, loving, and loveable. Today I am learning to give myself the unconditional love and acceptance I always wanted from people who didn't have it to give."
—*Al-Anon's Hope for Today*

Making This Practice My Own:

We can connect to others "for fun and for free" in many different ways.

- Find out your friend's favorite poet and read poetry aloud to her or him or send them a line from this poet on a postcard.

- Bring your friend her/his favorite music and listen to it with her or him.

- Share in the interests of another today: playing scrabble or chess, learning to knit or crochet with her/him, watching a sappy or slapstick video together.

- Make a photo album for the next person who invites you to a birthday party (after bringing a camera to the event and shooting lots of anonymous photos).

- Ask your oldest friend or grandparent about a memorable incident from her/his youth. Listen to what she/he tells you.

- Sing together.

- Laugh together.

- Meditate together.

- Ask your friend who is particularly quiet, if there is something that you could pray about for her or him.

Enough About ME, What do you think of ME?

"The fundamental problem is not alcohol [or any other person, place, or thing], we are told, but egocentricity—the mistaken belief that the ego is the center of one's being. The cause of our suffering, our sense of isolation, fear and anger at life, grows out of our egocentricity."—Philip Z.

Why do so many contemplatives—reflective types—I admire seem to emphasize the truism that comes from self-forgetting? Often such self-forgetting is sought through meditation or contemplating on whatever sense experience arises. This is the kind of attention that children give when they are in the throes of their imagination-in-play. Why is such concentration so elusive to most adults? So many of us, anyway, are often preoccupied with "how we're doing?" We rarely take time to just be with our lives, our world around us. We are more often wondering how we're performing and what you're thinking of our performance. Others of us feel tremendous lack in this regard and are busy trying to get it right or improve ourselves so we talk and talk about ourselves and our projects (projections of ourselves in the world) in an effort to find stable identities on which to stand...as if such a search actually could produce the diamond in the rough that we seek. So many of us want solid selves to be secure in, and the very framework we operate within betrays the pivot upon so much of the very same suffering from which we seek relief.

To meditate or pray is to sit still with the desire to see anew. We can cultivate fuller perspective precisely as we let go of the quest for finding the object that is called "self." What children do is concentrate with full attention and let their inner creator direct them. They rarely theologize or philosophize about the source of their inspiration; they, very simply, surrender to their imagination. They trust right direction will come as they love the game. Merton writes, "What in God might appear to us as 'play' is perhaps what God takes most seriously. When we are alone on a starlit night; when by chance we see migrating birds in autumn descending on a grove of junipers to rest and eat; when we see children in a moment when they are really children; when we know love in our own hearts, or when like the Japanese poet Basho says, "we hear an old frog land in a quiet pond with a solitary splash—such times the awakening, the turning inside out of all values, the 'newness,' the emptiness and purity of vision that makes themselves evident, provide a glimpse of the cosmic dance." But, many advise us to forget ourselves on purpose, cast-aside our solemnity to join in this playful dance. I'm with Philip Z. who says, "So long as we understand that the ego-self is only a part of who we are and not all that we are, we can develop a healthy and flexible ego. However, when we identify exclusively with our ego, we become disconnected from a deeper, more powerful aspect of ourselves. This other aspect of the human psyche is more encompassing, though less conscious part. This Higher Self or Higher Power is the true center of the psyche. By connecting with this larger aspect of ourselves, we discover our true nature. We realize that we have an ego, but we are not the ego."[14]

Making This Practice My Own:

- The next time you want something simple, say another cup of tea, take a few minutes to notice where the desire resides. Pay attention to the sensations in your body while following your breath. Do you still want the tea?

- Choose an object that you think you can't possible part with. Put it in a closet or the garage or attic or basement for one week. Did you miss it? After a couple of days, did you notice it wasn't there?

- If you become furious at someone, before you act make a list of all the bad qualities the person has. Then make a check mark next to each negative trait that you also share. Next, write down his/her good qualities. Make a check mark next to

---

[14] Philip Z., *A Skeptic's Guide to the 12 Steps* (Minneapolis: Hazelden, 1990).

those you have. Can you find some common ground?

Minding My Own Business

"Before Al-Anon, I had a false sense of self. Because of their diseases, my alcoholic father and my mother who grew up in an alcoholic home couldn't see themselves clearly. They weren't able to help me, either. As I grew up it seemed that my parents couldn't see me at all. I felt invisible and voiceless. I had no idea of my likes and dislikes, let alone what I would or would not accept in a relationship. I felt empty inside. When there did seem to be something inside me, it felt like someone else's experience."—*Al-Anon's Hope for Today*

When I hear the program of Al-Anon reminding me to "keep the focus on myself and my recovery and not on the alcoholic," it sometimes makes me angry. I think to myself: "He's the one with the alcoholism, he's the one with the emotional, physical, financial, social and professional identity problems—not me!" The Twelve-Step program of Al-Anon gives me the steps and the tools to focus on "keeping my side of the street clean." This means when my mate is overspending, overeating, overdrinking, and partying with his (under-drinking age) students, that I keep the focus on myself by asking myself, "What do I need for peace of mind right now?" and then, if I can, I attend to that need immediately.

Most importantly, I need to remember to mind my own business. His business is NOT my business. In many ways we can treat the running of our lives as if they were small businesses we are trying to run in socially responsible ways. I can't make him honor my rules, my job is to honor them myself. I need to see that so much of why he continues to slack in his business maintenance is because I'm hurting his chances to face the consequences of his actions. If he never gets to see the consequences of leaving the gas stove on, he never comes to realize what happens with his own inattention to details. More important than this habit of his is my bad habit of making his frailties and his blind spots the focus of my attention as if the most important thing I could do was to make the patriarch maintain his illusion of expertise. It's as if there's no God if I don't do my part to make him look the part of God. In so many ways my *Al-Anonic* ways become an ersatz religion, a false spirituality where "the alcoholic" is the focus for my serenity and security—where everything he does or doesn't do threatens to throw me off kilter. This craziness is the result of my misplaced loyalty to an external power—my husband.

The authentic power of rigorous honesty and courageous action in the world based on the conviction that a power within me, with the help of my community, can help me honor myself— as well as others' responsibility. I need not be afraid of what the alcoholic in my life will or will not do; he is not my deeper wisdom, he is not the force of all life cycles; he is not my inner compass. He has his own business to mind, as do I. I cannot run his unique business and he cannot run mine. The best we can do is share what works for us with genuinely curious others. I've found what works for me is to take my tentacles out of the alcoholic and use every arm of those tentacles to reach into myself for "a part of me that knows" what to do to most rewardingly show up for myself. It's good for me to discern what I need to do to take good care of my own physical needs by asking myself the following questions: "Do I need *physical needs*: food, rest, exertion, shelter, affection, community, or solitude?" As for my own *emotional-spiritual needs*—"Do I desire meditation, journaling, exercise, yoga, tea or a walk with a dear friend?" Or what about my *financial needs*?— "Do I need a second job that pays me what I need to live more comfortably as a single-home owner?" Or my *professional needs*—"Do I need to focus on doing whatever I am doing with fuller attention and preparation, being sure to show up in ways that my job demands (company picnics, advising lost students, outings, ceremonies, publishing, public speaking, community service, etc.)?"

Through greater awareness, I am realizing that no one else has my business as their top priority. No one else has nurturing and financially sustaining me (and my creative comforts) as their number one aim in life. Nobody else minds my business. They are too busy, appropriately, minding their own business.

An exercise that has helped me to mind my own business better is to listen to what bubbles forth during my 20-minute morning meditation. When I begin, I ask myself, "What needs minding in the store today?" I often get hints about what's being unattended to, and playtime is a big one.

Another big one is quiet time later in my hectic day; and finally, I get the hint that my mind machinery is getting all gunked up with hopeless-helpless negative thinking born of growing up in addiction, born of ancient fears that financial support simply must come from outside myself, or I'll never make it as a woman on my own. For about 15 years before she died, my grandmother used to scratch (and sniff?) the magic numbers on that Publisher's Clearing House scam, as if she'd never have enough money without a miracle windfall "from above." For years women have been taught to derive their security from someone or something outside themselves. We'll never have profit in our own lives if we don't take seriously the fact that our job is to mind our own businesses if we really want to taste what we are capable of creating.

Making This Practice My Own:
Revisit your earliest commitment in this book. What do I most love about my life as it is? How am I feeling about this area of my life? Is there any progress that I can see? List places where you
Revisit your earliest commitment in this book. What do I still struggle with in my life as it is? How am I feeling about this area of my life? Is

there any progress that I can see? List places where you are finding greater and greater acceptance of what you still struggle facing in your life.

*

*

*

*

*

*

No Longer Waiting for that Rescue Ship

"The world does not change as a consequence of our Twelve Step work. We are not promised divine intervention in the events of our life because of our devotion to God or because we proclaim *His* power and glory. Rather it is we who change—our attitudes and personalities are transformed so that we face life's challenges in new ways. Again, our new perspective comes not from some external God, but from our commitment to open ourselves to the deeper truths about the nature of reality and the human experience."—*Philip Z.*

"Most spiritual growth has come to me these past thirteen years through letting go of the belief that God (or anyone else) is or should be my *Daddy*."—*Jennifer M.*

"Nothing happened to you!" my dad *swore* to me when I confronted him after 20 years of remaining silent regarding his multiple cruelties towards me (and women in general). I responded with confidence, "Well then *nothing* sure left a lot of psychic damage, Pops."

One dreary night I fell in between sleep and wakefulness and started to tumble down into a dream. It was gray all over with a thick fog. I didn't know up from down. I could hear the lapping of waves hitting something and I realized that I was trying to stay afloat in a black-as-night ocean. It was hard to see my surroundings; there was only the lapping-water sound. I felt utterly alone and was getting tired of treading this icy-cold water. I remember hoping to see a lighthouse eventually to guide me to the direction of the shoreline. As I looked out on the horizon, it seemed infinitely bleak—I didn't know if there were other boats in the water; I couldn't see beyond a three-foot circle. I wasn't even certain I was moving forward or just riding with an undertow. All I did was fight the water to stay above its surface. My priorities were breathing, staying warm, and staying awake.

I'm not sure how much time had passed when I thought I heard and felt something moving toward me. It was almost like a muffled cowbell on the side of a boat—but how big was this boat?—I could only imagine. I fantasized about the boat, certain that it was coming to rescue me. Was it a steamer, like a battleship Loralie? Was it one of those big pontoon boats? I wondered how many people would be on the boat. Would there be other survivors who were once trying to stay afloat, just like me. Or would there be an intelligent investigator who was assigned to this rescue mission to find missing persons— disappeared at sea? Again, time was passing, but I wasn't sure how much time these fantasies had swallowed up. I did notice that the more I fantasized, the easier it was to ignore the slow-freezing of my muscles, now saturated with icy salt water. As the boat came closer, I knew it was a matter of time before I'd see what size it was and who was there. Soon, very soon, I'd be found. Soon, very soon, I'd be rescued.

Just then, something emerged from out of the dark fog. It looked like the bow of a large boat. I hoped the captain would see me and not run me over by mistake. As I tried to speak, to direct him, I felt salty water go down my throat, silencing me. I tried again to shout but all I could hear was my own whisper and ineffectual coughing out loud, "Over here!" The fog seemed like it was lifting now and I could make out that the boat was nothing more than a small dinghy—the kind of boat often attached to the back of bigger speed boats.

As the dinghy became clearer, I was hoping I was becoming more unmistakably visible to the one rowing it. I no longer called him captain now because anyone can row a dinghy, even the most-feeble child. I waved my hands wildly hoping he would see me by now; after all the fog seemed to be lifting more quickly. But, the boat's rower seemed to be ignoring me. I didn't understand this recalcitrant silence; it was just the two of us on a cold and dreary night; couldn't he see me nearly drowning? The boat seemed to go, ever so cruelly, right by me. I quickly started moving toward it as best as I could do so. I wanted to grab onto something but my legs and arms were on fire with prickly needles and going numb in the frigid waters. My limbs were on their last round of treading the water necessary to stay afloat. As I was feeling like this was going to be my last chance to be rescued, I seized on the stern of the boat with a force not even I knew was possible. It was a burst of adrenaline that enabled me to leap right on the back of the dinghy. When I did so, it tipped toward me as if it were empty. As I looked into it through salt-stung eyes, I saw, in fact, it was indeed empty.

Nothing was in it! The oars seemed to be strapped in well. I realized that it was the flailing oars and their metal holders that made the cowbell like ringing and the flapping water sound. I hoisted myself forward and into the boat and collapsed with exhaustion. All this time I'd been hoping for some outside rescuer, some seasoned captain, or knowledgeable coastguard to come find and save me. I felt so lost and so helpless for so long—it seemed. I'm now coming to see that life promises us nothing but opportunities to take action on our own (and others') behalf—we have many chances to learn to cultivate our own skills of being with whatever arises, with love.

Anthony de Mello says, "When we can see ourselves and others clearly, without projections, we will know what love is." He writes, "For you will have attained a mind and a heart that is alert, vigilant, clear, sensitive, a clarity of perception, a sensitivity that will draw out of you an accurate, appropriate response to every situation at every moment. Sometimes you will be irresistibly impelled into action, at others you will be held back and restrained. You will sometimes be made to ignore others and sometimes give them the attention they seek. At times you will be gentle and yielding, at others hard, uncompromising, assertive, even violent. For the love that is born of sensitivity takes many unexpected forms and it responds not to prefabricated guidelines and principles but to present, concrete reality. When you first experience this kind of sensitivity you are likely to experience terror. For all your defenses will be torn down, your dishonesty exposed, the protected walls around you burned.... As you begin seeing clearly, the hard, protective shell around your heart will soften and melt and your heart will become alive in sensitivity and responsiveness. The darkness in your eyes will be dispelled and your vision will become clear and penetrating and you will know at last what love is."[15]

---

[15] Anthony De Mello, *The Way to Love* (New York: Image Books, 1995).

Making This Practice My Own:

Mudita Practice

The companion practice of *karuna* or *metta* meditation is *mudita*, or sympathetic joy. *Karuna* is a pleasant tugging of the heart in response to suffering; *mudita* is joy at the good fortune of others. For some of us *karuna* is easy, while *mudita* is difficult. I think it has to do with how we feel about our own potential or lack of potential. When we encounter someone who is suffering, we might experience a subtle separation, a sense that we are better than the person who is suffering. When someone gets a job that we want or buys a nice car or home, we may feel that we are shortchanged. In both cases we feel separate. *Mudita* is a practice that opens our hearts further by helping us to know that there is enough for everyone. It is the antidote to jealousy and envy. Work with the phrase, "May your happiness and success never end," or "I wish you abundant joy" or "I wish you the very best!" Notice the change in mood after giving your thoughts to this aspiration for 10 minutes.

For example:

"May my ex-(former)partner have all the joy, success and happiness I seek."

Or

"May my hard-to-please boss find her/his worth today. May she/he be flooded with feelings of confidence and ease of being."

Or

"May my wealthy sister/acquaintance (Microsoft millionaire) be filled with all the love she seeks today, may she be blessed in every way possible."

Or

"May my least favorite politician be graced today with peace in his/her heart, and may this peace grow exponentially with each breath she/he takes."

Eating a Georgia Peach

Who would have thought a Yankee Buddhist from New York would have moved to Georgia to teach Christian Bible Studies and Christian Theology? Talk about biting into a Georgia peach! I thought I'd left Christianity behind when I left Princeton Theological Seminary—not with a whimper—but with a loud bang in 1988. It's an odd story. When I was a young Catholic girl of ten years attending Catholic mass every day of my life, I thought I'd been called to the priesthood. Mercy me, I didn't believe my parish priest when he warned me, "girls will never be priests!" I thought, "Why not? What's it take to practice for the priesthood? I could at least practice until I get it right, right?" I thought that being an altar boy would be a good place to begin. Again, Father Walsh said, "Altar BOY, altar BOY, Jennifer! Girls are NOT boys, therefore there are no girls who can be altar boys, right?" I did NOT understand. I was thoroughly convinced that I was "called" to be a priest! I was perplexed with his false discouragements and illogical, exclusionary conclusions. So I began to do the best I could to replicate a kind of priestly training of my own.

I gathered together a makeshift altar—an upside down TV-stereo box—in the corner of my bedroom. I covered this box with a lacey, eye-lit, tablecloth to give it the look I had seen every day at Church. I placed upon it a misselette or two (one to use to guide me and one to give away should another *lost soul* enter this holy place in need!), a white candle and a pink rosary that I had received at my first holy communion at age eight. I knelt in front of this altar every day to pray and contemplate God's silence. It felt quite natural to me, my calling. I was certain that Father Walsh was wrong and that, in time, he'd come to his senses.

Four years went by before I became disillusioned by the Roman Catholic Church's patriarchal stance. Everyday I worked harder and harder to fulfill my call. I did what I thought a good priest would do—I said an enthusiastic "yes" to service, and, anytime I could help another I would do so, often taking home runaways and latch-key kids, to my mother's chagrin. I resisted lying, cheating, and taking what wasn't mine—the stealing was something I'd actually been quite a pro at in terms of pilfering pennies or change from my alcoholic stepfather's pockets that hung limp in his closet. But my most memorable claim-to-priestly-fame was my vow to never swear and never allow such swearing in my presence without a corrective comment. Mercy, I was such a righteous little church lady (a euphemism for an Al-Anon) at age 13! I remember boys who were then called "hoods" who would try to goad me into swearing, promising me it wouldn't kill me to "take God's name in vain!" As time went on, my faith took a turn as my "calling" felt less and less assured. By age 14, I moved to a different town and came to the awareness that Catholic Churches everywhere were the same; there were no women priests allowed!

I'd originally thought such small-mindedness was due to my parish priest's old-world values and, therefore, unique to him. When I discovered the small vision in other Catholic Churches, that was **it** for me! I dropped out and hooked up with those hoods who said, "You'll live if you swear, just try it!" I did try swearing and other things too, especially booze, pot and sex. It all happened very quickly, almost like a reverse conversion experience. Then a few years later, at 16, under the weight of tremendous guilt for all my *sinful* behavior, I was urged by my Born-Again sister, Lotty, to "take Jesus Christ into my heart as my personal Lord and Savior." Lotty had left the Catholic Church and had been attending an Evangelical Church of God which taught her a more relaxed kind of faith where believers were saved by God's *grace* not their own effort-filled actions. She passed it on by saying, "Jesus will change you; there's nothing that you have to do but *receive* him." This was quite an alternative message than the one with which I had been raised as a Roman Catholic—each mass, before communion, one made a fist and beat their chest three times saying, "Lord (Lamb

134

of God), I am not worthy to receive you, only say the word, and I shall be healed."

As I wrestled with Lotty's version of what I called "a lazy man's faith," I decided, "It can't hurt to experiment!" I showered during the recitation of the prayer, in a way, offering myself a full-emersion Baptism. This gave me an experience of feeling hopeful that I could *be cleansed* from past mistakes and imperfections. I took to my newfound Protestant faith like Woody Allen in *Hannah and Her Sisters*. I went to their Bible, their revival meetings and heard all about the evil they saw in the world, especially in Russia! This was 1979, when every born-again Christian had read Hal Lindsey's 1984 prediction of Armageddon as God-ordained nuclear war between Russia and the Middle East. I heard it all and wondered how true it could be. Something in me (my critical mind?) remained a skeptical observer.

Later that summer, I found a more liberal Protestant church where they said I could be ordained. This pastor was like Martin Luther King, Jr. His sermons were not tirades against a non-Christian enemy. Rather, they were stories of inspiration that worked to build bridges of peace and understanding with the rest of the world. This was the kind of minister I wanted to emulate. This is the congregation that sponsored me to attend Seminary. While at seminary, I was expected to do field work at an inner-city Church for one year. My heart was not in the Church but in the places where the Church seemed afraid to go: prisons, AIDS clinics, homeless and battered women's shelters, etc. Those were the places my faith was truly tested and my *calling* was transformed into something quite different than what I had predicted.

After working with battered women as a chaplain for three years, I realized much of the Christian message seemed to be influencing the self-sacrificial behavior of the women I counseled.

The paternalism in the Church and within Christian theology also seemed to sponsor more passivity than self-care and seemed to inflict more harm upon these women than it seemed to help. So, after three years of giving it my all, I left the ministry and decided to study religion and religious motivations by doing my doctorate in Psychology of Religion. In my research, I was influenced by Gandhi's questions that ask: What helps and what hinders human progress within different religious traditions?

Making This Practice My Own: (set timer for 10")
After taking in a few deep breaths, and slowing down a little, imagine yourself to be sitting in a rocking chair or lying down in a hammock. What image can you conjure up that is soothing to you? Is it the quiet blue ocean that you are staring out onto or the warm expansive desert? Or is it the bright blue sky with clouds that fluff on past you? Let yourself rock in your chair or hammock. Rocking back and forth. Now, imagine a soothing sound or humming mantra.

Literally hear this sound: shalom, or *mushin* (no mind). If you can't hear it in your mind's eye or your middle ear, it's okay to say it aloud. Meditate on only this for 10 minutes. Quietly let your attention focus only on this sound and the inner clarity it can give you. Be open to what emerges. When the buzzer rings, bow with the question in mind, "What's my next step toward our highest good?"

"But I get REALLY Lonely!" from *The Cable Guy*

They have a saying in Alcoholics Anonymous and Al-Anon called "H.A.L.T." which means: "Never get too hungry, angry, lonely or tired." Lonely is a tricky one because I can just as easily avoid aloneness that can be appropriate solitude as I can isolate and become like Jim Carey's character "Chip Douglas" in *The Cable Guy* movie who, after attempting and failing suicide, says to his friend, "I get lonely sometimes." His "friend," whom he'd been stalking, empathetically comforts Chip by saying, "We all

138

get lonely sometimes, Chip." Chip responds with a desperate facial expression and says, "Yeah, but I get *really* lonely!" My experience of this "really lonely" feeling often comes up after having so much time with others that I'm exhausted; I have almost forgotten how to be alone in a constructive way. Sure, we all know how to be alone with some form of anesthetizing—with a pint of ice cream, a video, novel, or a glass or two of wine, or going to bed early to avoid feelings of utter aloneness. We all know how to be alone with something that knocks us out of awareness. But what about breathing in this aloneness instead of fighting it all the time…that's the real taboo!

The Tibetan Buddhist tradition teaches us to "see all experiences as the path to the wholeness we seek." There is no *nirvana* (release) without *samsara* (the continuous cycle of life, death and rebirth into suffering due to unconscious living). Everything we think is "shitty" and unacceptable about ourselves right now can be used as "fertilizer" for the fully perfect garden that is our lives—what the Dalai Lama calls "our original Buddha nature" or what Trungpa Rinpoche translates into "basic goodness." In terms of working with feelings of loneliness, it works well to breathe in these feelings as if breathing in dank air (like a dehumidifier) and exhaling, just as deeply, the ease of "being" that we seek.

What's the flipside of loneliness; what Alcoholics Anonymous' founder, Bill Wilson, calls "anxious apartness"? A full life? Contentment in solitude (*apart* from others) as well as with others (*a part* of a community). Another practice is to "extend compassion to all beings who feel just as trapped in the inability to relax in their own company as I do." This prayer is called *Karuna* or *Metta* in Sanskrit and it stands for extending loving kindness in all directions—starting with ourselves.

Where in your body are you holding back? What feeling needs acceptance before it will allow you to work with it? Where are you resisting being fully present in your life as it is, right now? Are you *really* lonely, like *Cable Guy's* Chip Douglas? Or are you hungry for something you can't imagine? Are you still angry about something or at someone? Are you really tired of the same old way of seeing your life? Do you feel stuck? Where in your body are you feeling this "stuckness"? Where in your body are you feeling your most primary feeling? Instead of fighting that awareness, you can welcome it: "May I find happiness and the root of happiness. May all beings who feel as lonely as I feel right now find true contentment, alone, as well as, with others. May we who feel so stuck find true ease of movement and the roots to this ease."

Breathing in this feeling and releasing this wish is the practice of *Metta* (Sanskrit for "loving kindness"). Breathing in this feeling and releasing its opposite is called *Tonglen* (Sanskrit for "taking and sending") and it is a form of exchanging self for other. These techniques are often used by

Tibetan Buddhists to cultivate *Bodhichitta* (Sanskrit for "open-hearted compassion") for all beings as well as a Bodhisattva vow to free all beings for happiness and to end their suffering and the roots of their suffering. All Bodhisattvas (Sanskrit for "awakened beings") elect to forgo the taste of nirvana until all beings taste nirvana—a final end to suffering. This is the most unselfish epitome of Mahayana Buddhism and is often misunderstood as masochistic behavior.

However, it is a form of embodying the truth of interdependence. We need look no further than the limited happiness of the very famous or very rich. They know their position is fragile; it's dependent on great numbers of people going without for their wealth or fame to exist at all. Distance, not likeness, creates such envy. This kind of positioning always produces a kind of emptiness born of isolation.

Making This Practice My Own:

Make a list of ten people you pity. How do I relate/respond to such people?
1.
2.
3.
4.
5.
6.
7.
8.
9.
10.

Make a list of ten people you envy. How do I relate/respond to such people?
1.
2.
3.
4.
5.
6.
7.
8.
9.
10.

Now ask yourself, what traits do I have in common with those I pity, those I envy? How are we alike? Here's an example of a situation I wish I could have handled with less resistance, less aggression, less passivity, less inertness.

What have I learned? How might I do one thing differently to respond/relate differently?

Focusing on What's Working

"We must be the change we wish to see in the world."—*Gandhi*

"To the extent that we ourselves are free of suffering, our very being becomes an environment in which others can be free of theirs, if it is the way of things."—*Stephen Levine*

"Prayer is not asking for things—not even for the best things; it is going where they are. The word, with its inevitable sense and stain of supplication, is therefore best abandoned. It is meditation and contemplation; it is opening another aperture of the mind, using another focus, that is the real creative process."
—*Gerald Heard*

I have heard many women living with alcoholics say, "I can't seem to hold my focus when my alcoholic partner is in the room." It's as if alcoholics are black holes whose disease of alcoholism sucks the life energy out of every living thing—even plants seem to wilt a little more rapidly in their presence. Okay, that last line has yet to be scientifically verified, but ask most people living with alcoholics or those with untreated illnesses and they will tell you, "living things seem to die more quickly in this house!" So how do the loved ones of such people hold their focus? What exercises can they do to remain connected to their inner focus, inner direction? "We all have inner compasses," according to all spiritual traditions and silence and attention seem to be the two antennae that we can use to tune into this guidance.

So few of us have unfettered lives where we can just find time to sit quietly each day and focus. But, when we do make the time to reflect or get quiet, there's great insight that can bubble forth—a third way of seeing whatever we need to face, accept, or address with new eyes. What techniques work? Psychologist Eugene Gendlin has worked with the concept call "focusing."

Focusing

Making This Practice My Own:

In this practice, we seek to get comfortable in a room where we can remain undisturbed or undistracted. We sit upright while we take in at least three minutes of deeper breathing without any discursive thoughts or inner narrative running through our minds.

Gendlin suggests looking at a timer so we get a sense how long three minutes actually takes to pass. Then he invites us to ask ourselves, "How am I doing right now? Is everything alright for me just now?" Usually, what will emerge will come in the form of a familiar mental tape that will say something specific about old angst or problems with people in our lives or worries about upcoming meeting our responsibilities, etc. Gendlin then asks us to set aside all of that for now. We can pick it back up if we want to after this exercise, but, for now, we want to get a deeper appreciation for the *felt sense* of our experience in our bodies. We want to focus in on this *felt sense* and see what it is saying to us—hear what it needs from us, more specifically. What is the feeling? Is it a tightness, soreness, jumpy-tenseness, or lethargic heaviness? Is it sticky, hot, hard or soft? What is its nature? What is the quality of the feeling? Again, Gendlin is not asking what is the source of the feeling but what is the *quality* of the *felt sense*?

As I do this practice myself, I notice a clenched feeling of bracing myself against life's disappointments, today, as I acknowledge that my marriage is on its last legs. But for this exercise, I stay only with the *felt sense* of "Hazy, jumpy-tightness." I set aside the narrative association to my marriage and stick with the feelings. Next, I ask, "What would make the *felt sense* feel better right now? What does the *felt sense* need?" This part can be wildly imaginative—it need not be possible in real time or at all. Does it wish to be carried away by a spaceship? Does it need a bath where it can melt down the tight, muscular feelings that feel so swollen, so sore?

What would honor the *felt sense* right now? Give it three minutes and see. Really allow for it to speak for itself; don't force an answer, because that's not going to work for the *felt sense*. What would make the hazy-tenseness lessen or become clearer and loosen up? Give it its time to answer. Does it need a battalion of guardians to invisibly surround it with shields and laser stun-guns facing outward to all potential threats? Does it need an inner-spirit to pump it up at the inner-spirit gas station? What would take the best care of this *felt sense* right now? And then, we can keep going on like this. After this first round, we can move on to round two and start at the top.

After all this, we can ask ourselves, "Am I feeling completely better, and is everything just right with me now?" Let your *felt sense* answer—where is some residual shifting going on? Now that can be the new place to focus in and ask, "What is the quality of this *felt sense* and what does it need from me right now?" When we've had enough of this exercise for today, it's best to stop and get on with what's next today. Observe what kind of physical-emotional relief follows this exercise. For more on this kind of work, see Eugene Gendlin's book entitled, *Focusing*.[16]

Bottomless Pits

"Sometimes the things that bother us most about others are the very things we do ourselves without realizing it."—*How Al-Anon Works*

"Healing starts when I stop asking, "Why me?"—*Hope for Today*

"I therefore resolve to stop blaming the alcoholic for what is beyond his or her control—including the compulsion to drink. Instead, I'll direct my efforts where they can do some good: I will commit myself to my own recovery."
—*Courage to Change*

Today, August 28th, 2002, I just signed my divorce papers and I am feeling pretty good, considering that this is divorce number two for me. I remind myself that "the only true mistakes are the ones from which we learn nothing." I'm

---

[16] Eugene T. Gendlin, *Focusing* (New York: Bantam, 1982).

trying to remember another very important, if not, classic, lesson: Unless I deal with my own sense of feeling like an empty well inside, I'll continue to attract men who are bottomless pits. Why do we invite life to mirror our own blind spots? Is it because we are too afraid to face alone these cracks in ourselves? Do we really think that two cracked mirrors are better than one…that two children of alcoholics will face life more responsibly than one? What I found is that both Richard and I were eager to hide behind the shortcomings of each other. He could distract himself with finding flaws in my character, education, values, or cloying behaviors with others. I know it was easier to avoid my own shortcomings and instead lose myself with delicious worry over his excess drinking, eating, spending and cruel humor around others—he truly collected the inappropriate!

When I asked Richard to move out of our home (about one full year after our beautiful Buddhist wedding), I thought the chaos and bottomless pit of *his* needs would go away too. I didn't realize that the absence of his shame and destructiveness would leave me to face my own without a buffer of another being on whom I could project my own. This is scary for me—facing my own emptiness, my own chaos, my own obstacles to growing up—cultivating self-responsibility along with a sense of humor!

Moving the primary addict out of the home left me to face my own addictions to various escapes. Why does my "aloneness" produce loneliness? Must time with myself feel like such a bottomless pit? What can we do to address this sense of hollowness within ourselves?

My experience shows me that resisting the pit only prolongs, deepens and widens it. So now, what do we do? Breathing in the feelings we fear as the earlier chapters remind us, gives perspective like never before. It also allows us to feel the space around the feelings that feel so overwhelming, so fixed, so real. I'm aware that everything in most of us wants to resist these feelings as if they were hot flames. If breathing feels impossible to do—allow yourself another activity to do with it. This can help those of us who feel that sitting still is not an option.

Drawing and breathing or writing and breathing or singing or dancing or breathing while doing Yoga, Tai Chi or Qi Gong all work as forms of meditation. Any movement with one-pointed attention on the breath will eventually produce the calm we "bottomless pits" are seeking.

One idea that helps me is to realize that if I magnetize bottomless pits to me, I may have my own version of a "black hole of need" hidden from myself. This is scary to fathom, especially because it feels more manageable to think, "the truly needy ones are way over there." But we don't tap into our authentic power until we are able to take stock of our own blind spots and secret shame. When we're fearless at looking honestly at our own tendency to suppress needs, we'll start to see, little by little, how this imbalance in ourselves attracts people to us who are out of whack with needs and looking for our suppression-style temperament to fix them. We choose these people and they choose us with the idea (which comes way down deep in our being) that "we can help each other find homeostasis." "We can heal together." "We can balance out each other." These are the sentences that flood us with euphoric feelings of "true love" in the beginning of our bonding. These are the feelings of hope mixed with fantasies of a whole or perfect future together—we gracefully exchange the give and take of unconditional love. This is the illusion part of romantic coupling.

The red flags of "save me!" are well-tucked away under the blankets of denial and romantic fantasies that seem to keep us cozy and warm, for now. Those red flags might shoot up, or jut out, in some way or another, as time goes by, but, if the denial is thick enough, we'll see them as flags that are waving us in for a safe landing!

The "fantasy self" or "false self" that we project out into the world wants to see what she or he needs to see, and this will work for awhile. Disillusionment will occur eventually, especially with daily time together. Realistic working with the bottomless pits in ourselves and tolerating, with compassion, the bottomless pits of others will have to be cultivated if we want deeper knowing and deeper peace.

"How ready and willing am I today to invite the transforming power of acceptance into my will and my life? Each day is a new beginning.... We can learn to accept ourselves and become willing to change our attitudes for the better."
—*Blueprint for Progress*

"Acceptance is the answer to all my problems today" says AA's founder, Bill Wilson.

Making This Practice My Own:
How do I practice this acceptance?

In practice, the term *acceptance* means temporarily suspending judgments of right and wrong. It implies a kind of flat, non-evaluative willingness to just let things be, regardless of whether or not they seem fair, desirable, or convenient. Full acceptance—choosing life in its entirety—is the key to serenity. It is also the essence of the middle way as it relates to your everyday existence. When I talk about choosing life, I mean choosing everything that exists and everything that can be thought about, including inanimate objects and abstractions, like death or gods/goddesses, or any other characters you might think about. Even thoughts such as "I cannot possibly accept that!" are included.

If your life includes everything you know about or think about, and you agree to accept life unconditionally, then you are agreeing to accept everything you perceive to be happening, from the very best to the very worst. Actually, the enlightened person recognizes that both good and bad are necessary threads in life's fabric. Your acceptance is a statement of uncompromising inclusion.[17]

This week I will chant this affirmation for 10" each morning and see what I notice about my mood/day.

ACCEPTANCE CHANT:
"I boldly and courageously affirm and choose life unconditionally. I accept all of it as perfect however it happens to show up today." At the end of 10", open your eyes slowly with a bow.

Mercury Pools

"They must often change, who would be constant in happiness or wisdom."—*Confucius*

"We never step in the same river twice."
—*Heraclitus*

"When in the sea of Buddha, know that there is no sea, and no Buddha, and no in."—*Rich Walter*

---

[17] David Gregson & Jay S. Efran, *The Tao of Sobriety: Helping Your to Recover from Alcohol and Drug Addiction* (New York: St. Martin's Press, 2002).

Swirling mirrors are in constant motion—as I look into them I realize that they will not let me see my reflection for long. Just when I think I've found it, "My identity is this way or that way," the image melts into another pool of mercury. "I" cannot be pinned down. "I" am not a thing! "I" am never fixed, but am as lively and dynamic as any living creature in its lifecycle.

The search for a permanent, abiding self or an unchanging identity that feels comfortably predictable is an invitation to suffering. Such desires for absolute self-knowledge have driven many persons mad. Buddhists and Hindus alike say, "Because we are living beings we are interdependent with all other living beings." When we operate optimally, we operate in generosity of spirit, compassionate truth-telling, and peaceful acceptance of the realities we need to deal with and respond to, together.

To try to find contentment by grasping for a fixed sense of ourselves—so that we can know who we are in every situation, thus trust that we'll have integrity and therefore like and respect ourselves—is to operate out of what a Chinese friend of mine calls "rock logic." Rock logic always seeks solidity, hard facts, permanence, fixed knowledge, consistent behavior and beliefs. Rock logic—when operating—always tries to be right, to be the last argument standing, to intimidate with its huge firmness. But, Daoist lessons often entail the wisdom of "water logic." Water logic flows constantly, works with and around obstacles, carries and softens whatever falls into its watery nature. It also erodes, ever so gently, the illusion of fixedness and impenetrable nature of all rocks in its path, from the smallest grains of sand to the largest rock formations on earth. Water is as powerful as it remains fluid and flexible.

Self, or identity, truly is a temporary constellation that is conceptually or heuristically useful. It helps us to have wishes that translate into goals that invite us to risk engagement in life. For instance, when we were little, it helped us for a moment even as much as a year or two to ask, "What do I want to be when I grow up?" We'd gather together ideas, myths and fantasies and let our imaginations carry us into the future where we'd see and meet people who did work we admired: firefighter, photographer, painter, pianist, priest, cowgirl, cop, or school teacher. We'd try on these mantels by acting them out or dressing the part. These games gave us a taste of this role but the role-playing was flexible, informative and fun. We switched easily from cowgirl to cop to exotic dancer with not much worry about identity loss—no fanfare.

Today, to imagine several dream work situations or vocations can cause tremendous anxiety—as if our lives depended on sameness—as if our current work was the final expression of our true selves, our true identity. Such rigidity is born of fear and dullness to the dynamic flow of life that creatively runs through us always and seeks fluid and regular discharge or expression. Trying to pin ourselves down to one fixed role only produces depression via stagnation. Saying "yes" to the flow of life is saying "yes" to not knowing what will come next. After all, we, like life, are dynamic, changeable, mysterious and ongoing— this can be a cause for celebration once we've made the framework shift that appreciates "water logic" over "rock logic."

When we make this *perspectival* shift, we open up to embracing life's ups and downs as forces not unlike the natural seasons and rhythms of nature of which we, as humans, play only a small part. Loosening our desire for fixed identities is often called "a breakdown" in the West and "a breakthrough" in the East...nothing to be feared only welcomed with the 10,000 things.

Making This Practice My Own: (set timer for 10")
Ask this one question with every in breath and ask it again with every out breath: "Who am I now?" When the timer rings, take a bow of thanks.

Bodhisattva's Values

"None of us is free until all of us are free."
—*Gandhi*

What values are celebrated in Buddhism? According to the Dalai Lama, the Bodhisattva Avolokitesvara called the "Goddess of Infinite Compassion" is the highest human form in the Mahayana branch of Buddhism. She is the pinnacle achievement of enlightened human behavior. She has made the supreme sacrifice to forego her own release from the cycle of suffering, rebirth and death until all beings are freed from this cycle (called *samsara*). She forgoes *nirvana*—that awakened state of the Buddha. Consequently, her presence on earth is to extend compassion to all suffering the mistaken view born of grasping (clinging to what we desire) or aversion (pushing away what we don't desire). She spends her whole life modeling right view/responsiveness and developing non-self centered seeing. Many have twinned her with the

Roman Catholic Church's cult of the Virgin Mary, imagining her to be long-suffering, self-sacrificial and a caregiver of all God's children. If we were to step in a Buddhist temple and walk behind the wall where the Buddha is displayed (normally, the northern-most wall), the Bodhisattva would be on the other side of Buddha's teaching in the world. She often has people bowing and lighting incense to her for their human sufferings of illness, sick children, and wayward relatives. She is thought to heal others into right action.

What is the force of the Bodhisattva's healing power? Is it the same as the empathic mother Mary of Roman Catholicism? Is it tantamount to Jesus' miracles through the laying on of hands and calling upon God's power? The tales of how the Bodhisattva brings an end to suffering for others are told over and over by 14th Century

Buddhist scholar, Shantideva. These Buddhist stories were told as far back as the 7th century.[18]

A striking nuance to every tale is how the Bodhisattva will take on the shape and style of whatever being she's here to help. She'll morph to make sense to that particular person in their unique place in space and time. If having sex with the suffering other would help that other achieve enlightened awareness of their own impermanence or the transient nature of all desire, the Bodhisattva would do so—especially in the Tantric versions of her work in the world.

Making This Practice My Own:
What is one thing I can do today that is just a hair different from my regular approach? Can I drive to work a brand new way? Can I eat an hour later or an hour earlier than I usually eat? Can I call someone who I haven't spoken to for a while and ask for her/his advice about

---

[18] See Shantideva's *The Way of the Bodhisattva*, (Boston: Shambhala Press, 2003).

approaching a particular problem I'm struggling with?

- Walk backwards at least once today?

- Be willing to think about a political position or religious conviction that is not your own? Try to see how someone with the best intentions might see it that way?

- What if I were the "other" gender, how might I feel about my chosen profession or body/self-image? How might I begin and end this day?

- Ask your postal worker, your janitor, local math teacher or gym teacher, or an office temp how they would approach the dilemma with which you're currently struggling.

- Pretend your 80 or 8 years old. Now write a letter to yourself at the age you really are now. What advice does that 80/8 year old have to share with you about what really matters?

Being the True Warrior in Times of War and Peace

"The root of war is how we live our daily lives."—*Thich Nhat Hanh*

In Buddhism, according to one ancient source, a story is told again and again about our essential interrelatedness through the tale called "Net of Indra"—this symbol is often described as a net of jewels, each of which reflects all others and itself.

For Tibetan teacher, Trungpa Rinpoche, a true warrior struggles to remain vulnerable. She or he fights to remove any pretense of armor and walks through life fully-engaged and fully open-hearted. He often used a metaphor of "soft spot" as an example of that place within us that feels so vulnerable to life's pains and losses. He said we can be brave and stay open—this is the courage to cultivate awake-ness, this is the balm to 21st century ills of alienation, war, and all the other "isms" born of ignorance, fear and rejection of our own vulnerability. We only reject in the other what we hate in ourselves.

If we can make peace with the ever-present pinch of tenderness of our own soft-spot, we can walk through anything with fearlessness. This is the kind of warriors the 21st century needs to sustain life on this planet. This is the kind of courage we need to cultivate rather than attending one more Kung Fu-like seminar for self-improvement and securing tough exteriors. This soft spot will be helped by accenting its universality. This means honoring the fact that even your worst enemy in life has such tenderness under their cruel exterior. This means whoever hurt you most was probably also as hurt by someone else and so on and so forth. All cruelty is born of rejecting our own and another's tenderness.

As Twelve-Steppers say, "Hurt people, hurt people." Right now there are approximately three-dozen civil wars being fought on planet earth (that's one out of every five nations). We might think that the last thing we conscious citizens should be cultivating is peace with our own vulnerability. But that's just it, we cannot afford NOT to awaken the rejection of our own vulnerability; such rejection is killing us! We reject our tender interdependence on this planet when we don't recycle, when we spray pesticides, when we tolerate unethical globalization practices in business (practices that don't protect worker's rights and health needs), when we shoot steroids into animals and eat them and then wonder why cancer rates are doubling, we obsess about how Arab countries treat "their" women when in our own (presumed *free* U.S.) homes, one-third of women are beaten, molested, raped and sometimes murdered by the very men who claim to love and protect them.

We cannot afford to neglect and reject such tenderness. These feelings of vulnerability tie us to each other—they need not be purged into violence and ethnic-cleansing, racial segregation, homophobic violence and sexist practices that cripple freedoms to make a living wage. It's catching up with us, this rejection; it's showing up in excessive consumption that is non-sustainable and non-renewing. What can one person do to push back this tidal wave of greed, ignorance and hatred of various kinds? Some have chosen to become Bodhisattva warriors.

We can cultivate compassionate awareness of our interdependence. Every action we take in our day affects another…and is affected by the actions of others. The coffee we drink is grown in Costa Rica or Panama, the clothes we wear were most likely made in China or Malaysia for the equivalent of $3.00 a day and the cars we drive were constructed in Japan, Korea, etc. Not one action we take do we generate solely for ourselves, affecting only ourselves, as so many of us believe. With awareness of our interdependence we would never act with such carelessness and grandiosity, as if there were no consequences to our consumption.

With sensitive awareness that we cultivate every day, we might think we'd cripple ourselves with guilt and paralyze ourselves with fear of hurting each other or the planet with "one more wrong move." An offshoot of Hinduism is Jainism.[19] In this tradition it is often that one will sweep before they walk so as not to kill any unsuspecting microbes. So should we be like the Jains, should we resist moving altogether so as not to harm anyone? Jains, like Hippocrates or

---

[19] *Ahimsa* and *Anekäntväd* (non-violence and multiplicity of views) are the basis and the life-force of Jainism. All other Jain philosophies are branches off these two main philosophies. Major fundamentals of non-violence are: 1) all living beings are equal, 2) every living being wants to live and does not want to die, 3) every living being wants to be happy and does not like pain and 4) you treat others the way you like to be treated. The practice of non-violence is judged by one's intentions and deliberate actions. If a person deliberately and knowingly harms other living beings, then it is violence. But if involuntarily or in unavoidable circumstances, some insects are killed, then it is an exceptional situation. Whether it is by our actions, or by our speech or in our thoughts, hurting others without any specific reason is *himsa* - violence. See also *The Fundamentals of Jainism* by Harendra Shah, http://www.jcnc.org/jainism/reference.asp

the Dalai Lama's honor the motto, "Do no harm." But what's fearless about that?

Fearlessness is doing the lesser harm and walking out there—fully engaged—anyway. We can't please everybody and to try to do so is to come from the wrong framework. We're here to contribute for the sake of all of us—there's no one in particular to please and there's no one in particular who needs to be singularly pleasing when we're all cultivating peaceful warrior status in times of war. Such open-heartedness is only for the truly fearless. Such activity will have its cost but full living cannot be purchased in any other way.

Making This Practice My Own:
Revisit your earliest commitment in this book. What do I most love about my life as it is?

- How am I feeling about this area of my life? Is there any progress that others (or I) can see? List places where you are finding greater and greater acceptance in your life.

- Revisit your earliest commitment in this book. What do I still struggle with in my life as it is? How am I feeling about this area of my life? Is there any progress that I can see? List places where you are finding greater and greater acceptance of what you still struggle facing in your life.

Happiness—It's Never Too Late!

"Serenity isn't a matter of chance; it's a matter of choice. The best of all possible gifts is a tranquil mind. You can't go out and buy it. You have to earn it for yourself…"—*Al-Anon Forum Favorites*

"My life is my message."—*Mahatma Gandhi*

"Whatever you wish for yourself, wish the same for others."—*Bhagavan Mahavira*

As I meditate this morning, I am starting to feel what I'm looking for—a deeper sense of surrendering to a wiser self than my small or narrow self thinking in the world. It's like melting into the marshmallow man or a child falling into a bean bag chair until she's totally enveloped. In a way, all mystical experiences speak of such small self—or ego—overcoming through union with the divine or divinities of some form. This is brand new to experience such merging or emersion into a wiser self.

Self-trust is something children of alcoholic or abusive homes rarely cultivate. It's too scary! Violence—or acting out in some fashion—was often the result. We never knew that such violence and drinking was not caused by our behavior nor did we know that "perfect" behavior could not control, cure, or contain it. But it was too late; as kids, we already thought some kind of hyper-attunement to others would make us safe. We didn't know better until these habits had *become* us. The good news is that it is never too late to wake up. It's never too late to invite happiness and a higher consciousness into our hearts and minds. It's never too late to let hope/life/love push us out of inertia and self-involvement, shame and harmful focuses. We can help each other snap out of such narrow-self-thinking.

Perfectionism, isolation and shame dissolve under the warmth of true friendships. Such kindnesses melt rigidities of all kinds. Such kindness starts with prayer and meditation practices that we begin practicing with ourselves. As you wake up, pee and splash water on your face (not to be mixed up!), find a place to sit up right for 10 minutes of quiet contemplation. This solitude is a time of stating your wishes for self and others. In Sanskrit, it's called *Maitri* or "loving kindness" meditation. It starts with self and moves outwards. "Today, may I find happiness and the roots of happiness? Today, may I find an end to suffering and the roots of the end of suffering?" It goes on: "May my loved ones find happiness and the root of happiness. May they know the end of suffering." And lastly: "May those with whom I've heretofore had trouble loving find happiness and its roots and the end of suffering and its roots." These stated intentions change all persons involved and most dramatically change us. Give it a try for 90 days—each morning for 10 minutes. See what happens. Even the most skeptical scientist knows the value of experimenting.

Making This Practice My Own: (set timer for 10")
Sit or lie in a position that you can hold comfortably. Close your eyes if you like and take a couple of really deep breaths, feeling your breath going in and out and noticing your chest rising and falling. Now bring your attention to the top of your head and wish your head well.

May my mind be clear and spacious like the sky, may all negative thoughts and feelings and dis-*ease* drift away like clouds. May my mind be filled with ease, well-being, and serenity. Imagine this feeling of well-being (as if it were a cool breeze) moving down your face—around your eyes, your nose, your cheeks, and moth so that all the muscles of your face begin to soften and relax. Imagine the coolness of well-being moving into your jaw, down your neck, across your shoulders, down your arms, and into your hands and fingers, so that the top part of your body feels light and easy. Let the relaxation flow down your back, vertebra by vertebra, washing away any tightness or prickly hot tension. Let the relaxation radiate through your chest, around your heart, in your stomach so that all knots are untied and everything is soft and easy. Let the well-being move through your hips, down your legs, into your feet and toes.

Take a moment to enjoy all the warming muscles of your body working together in harmony, with no tightness and no tension. Take a couple of really deep breaths, being aware of your breath going in and out, feeling your chest rising and falling. Now visualize yourself as you are now or at some other tender time in your life. Take the image of yourself, place it in your heart, and surround it with care and tenderness. When the timer rings, let yourself say this *Metta* or Buddhist loving-kindness aspiration for someone you care about or struggle with:

May _____ be safe and protected.

May _____ be happy and peaceful.

May _____ be strong and healthy.

May _____ take care of myself with joy.

When You're Rowing a Boat with Only One Oar

A while ago, I came to the realization that having an obsessive-compulsive problem—when we think that *thinking* about our fear will help diminish its impact on us—is tantamount to rowing a boat with one oar. It may make us feel like at least we're in motion, at least we're doing something! But, the truth is, spinning around in circles is not a viable solution to our obsessive concerns. We may be moving molecules but we're going nowhere in particular. When the mind is caught up in this kind of obsessive worry, the last thing the mind can do is see its own caught-up-ness; it is blind to its habitual patterns of thinking.

What seems to interrupt this perpetual, unrewarding cycle, what Buddhists call *Samsara*? More often than not, I have to see the failure of this old habit in the act of failing me. I have to "hit bottom" or go over the edge of the waterfall that I've been rowing around in circles trying to avoid. If I could have awakened sooner, I am certain that I would have. In my own case, I have had to crash my mental boat several times before getting the message that I'll have a much better chance of working with the rapids if I have two oars in the water. Just "one oar" is what it looks and feels like when I try to solve my anxieties about life as an adult by my habitual mental machinations. If I can integrate my inner-wisdom—my Buddha Nature, or Higher Power, or God's-eye-view, harmonize with the Dao or however your spiritual tradition renders it—I'm on the road to a more manageable future. By "more manageable" I don't mean a future without struggle, obstacles, tragedies, or losses. Rather, I mean one that includes clearer seeing with the help of spiritual support through what Twelve-Steppers call, "working with life on life's terms."

When I'm in mental-machination land, it's very much like guilty masturbation—when I'm all alone and not able to trust the fact that I have the capacity to bring my raw experience to a safe relationship. I don't have to do this alone—it's one way but not the only way and surely not the best way every time. Now, I'm not knocking masturbation; as Woody Allen says, "It's sex with someone I love!" Rather, I'm using mental masturbation as a metaphor for frustrating isolation and fear of greater intimacy that, at different times for different people, can show up in the form of years of masturbation-only sex lives. For me, trusting the intimacy of a safe spiritual ally is tantamount to having sex. It's scary at first, but so great afterwards. It can't be described with my intellect alone because such intimacy is born of heart language and sharing of this kind arouses raw feelings.

In the West we call this our "heart language" or the language of intimacy but in Buddhist cultures they have a term "heart-mind" (*Citta* in Sanskrit, *Xin* in Chinese, *Shin* in Japanese) which can mean the same source of basic goodness—the place where our original nature germinates and is born.

Many meditation techniques in Tibetan Buddhism focus on *Bodhicitta* or awakening our Buddha-heart-mind that empathizes, skillfully, with others and with our own situation. When we feel our own rawness and don't pull into ourselves like turtles or hermit crabs retreating into their hard shells they call home. Instead, we move out of ourselves, courageously, into fuller relationships with people and all things. So many of us think we prefer the hard shell of a hermit crab's castle—but usually such choices to stay encased in that armor are born of our helpless fear and hopeless sadness. We adjust to our "small selves" and stay in our armored vaults rather than risk the potential burn of our tender hearts. And yet, this is like rowing with one oar—mind without heart—it gets you nowhere. It only gives you the illusion of moving towards safety.

Ironically, mental concentration without emotional knowledge actually increases our overall weakness and fosters insensitivity to our surroundings and this imbalance of focus can really put us at risk. Such one-oared rowing leaves us even more vulnerable to dangers and experiences that would be more wisely faced with full mind-body attunement.

"My habit is to go the one-oar route, I can't help myself!" most of us cry. It's true that we are unable to help ourselves most effectively when we're working alone. "Same-mind solution, same-mind problem." That's why we need spiritual friendships to help us carve out the attention we crave and the direction we need to best listen to the heart-mind in concert. In time we will grow to be superbly balanced in heart-mind cultivation and instead of ditching our friends because "now we got it and are good to go out on our own," we'll never want to return to the one-oared technique, practiced solo, ever again. We'll love solitude but will know that loving communion is the true catalyst to risk-taking. Rawness, our original self, cannot be uncovered in isolation. We need to delicately and compassionately *unwrap* each other. In time, we will be eager to take off the heavy burdens of old armor and old techniques that are no longer in service of our emotional evolution.

Making This Practice My Own:

Be willing to look up a support group in your area (any anonymous group of your choosing or ask a therapist to recommend a support group to you that could help you). Give the different meetings 6 tries before you decide to keep going or not.

Be willing to look up a meditation or prayer group in your area—any denomination is fine as long as love (not hate) is the message and they do NOT demand money from you to be a member. Give the different meetings 6 tries before you decide to keep going or not.

Be willing to look up an environmental education group in your area—Sierra Club (online or in your phonebook) can give you references for nature hikes, bird watching groups, or bicyclists in your area. Give the different meetings six tries before you decide to keep going or not.

Let Go and Let River

"Our lives are nothing more than a single drop in the flow of a mighty river. Together with an infinite number of other drops, we form that river, and we flow steadily and surely to the sea. At times we leap, we sing; at times we move silently toward the sea. We have reached the time to look back over the last years, which we spent desperately pursuing a dream of scaling the peaks, and reflect on the truth that we are flowing gently to the sea, from where we will return to the skies. Our only choice, I believe, is to start over from that realization."
—*Hiroyuki Itsuki*

There are times in my life when I've felt pinched in a corner, feeling helpless about which way to turn next. Should I move to the new town, start that new job, enjoy that next relationship, buy that new house, car, etc.? Or should I just appreciate where I am, enjoy what I have in front of me, take better care of the people, places, and things in my present life? These are times many Twelve-Steppers say, "Let go and Let God." I envy them their faith. I've seen it work for them with my own eyes! But, I'm a Buddhist who does

183

not believe in a personal God. I believe that the only power in the universe that we can count on is change and, from where I stand, change seems to be quite impersonal, neutral, and never about me (never for or against me, either). So it's irrational to rest in the idea that letting go is going to always be a sure benefit to all concerned. After all, life's processes include me but are, in the end, not about just me.

I say, "Let go and let river" and I say this based on my experience of rivers. The pre-Socratic, Greek philosopher, Heraclitus says, "We never step into the same river twice." We don't get to hold time still. We don't get guarantees in life, we only get change and it's a 50-50 kind of change. Life could go this way or it could go that way. There's no guarantee that "letting go" means we get our wishes to come true. We are but one drop in the river that is constantly in motion...together with an infinite number of other drops: we make up this entire river. We can let go and see what happens or continue to fight the flow. Which will you choose?

Making This Practice My Own:

Zen Master Thich Nhat Hanh taught this exercise when I was at Plum Village, France. Go to the nearest park in your area and commit to silent walking/breathing for 20 minutes. Here's what to say with every step and ever "in" breath: "As I breathe in, I have arrived." Here's what to say with other step and every "out" breath: "As I breathe out, I am home."

"As I breathe in, I have arrived. As I breathe out, I am home." After the timer stops, take a bow of gratitude for your journey is just beginning.

NOTE TO READER

"What is to give light must endure burning."
—*Victor Frankl*

Dear Reader:

After writing this book, I realize that by embracing life in all its pain, sorrows, grief and loneliness, I also get to experience the depths of joy, ecstasy, love and intimacy. So much has improved for the better and this is the primary paradox of all wisdom traditions, including the Twelve Steps.

But, as we listen to the nightly news, we often hear that so many people, in the name of their religions, seem determined to destroy the "other" or whomever they deem "not us." So many sad and fear-filled people, in the name of their religion, seem hell-bent on destroying all sense of delight, all sense pleasures, all instincts born of desire—Nietzsche claims that it is precisely this kind of asceticism that produces "sick priests" and "anemic animals," not creatures with a spirit of spontaneity, self-trust, or enlivening engagement.

Nietzsche predicted that such withholding from ourselves, as our religion, would have a tremendous backlash in violence—the opposite of the love the founders may have intended. Violence cannot be turned inward without it also being turned outward...it is contagious that way. We cannot kill another without losing our sibling and because we are alienated from a sense of family with all sentient beings, we are tempted to destroy each other, what we fear, in search of our own oblivion. Some call such systematic habits of self-other aggression a "disease." It is in this sense of disease that I understand addictions.

Addictions seem to be our way of masking our own unfelt aggression and hunger for "right" connections to ourselves and others. Addictions express our hopeless feelings that "things will never improve, life is unfair, people/leaders disappoint me so I may as well anesthetize or find my own escape."

After spending years and years in the rooms of Twelve Steps Anonymous, practicing its principles as I understand them, and cultivating my own practice of mindfulness meditation and social engagement in my community, I found I wanted to share the way I bring together these diverse wisdom traditions. Yes, this book is a personal philosophy or spiritual autobiography, and yes, you may find much that some of these stories resonate with your own. Perhaps insights that arise might take you in a new direction all together or affirm the practices you already value. But, when sparks of thought ignite, they can invite dialogue. Please know that I welcome such dialogue on my interactive webpage:

www.mylifedesignunlimited.com

May you find what you need and want what you find!

Jennifer Manlowe
Bainbridge Island, WA

Suggested Reading

William Alexander, *Cool Water: Alcoholism, Mindfulness and Ordinary Recovery* (Boston: Shambhala, 1997).

Mel Ash, *The Zen of Recovery* (New York: J.P. Tarcher, 1993).

Madeline Ko-i Bastis, *Peaceful Dwelling: Meditations for Healing and Living* (Boston: Tuttle Publishing, 2000).

Thomas and Beverly Bien, *Mindful Recovery: A Spiritual Path to Healing from Addictions* (New York: John Wiley and Sons, 2002).

Pema Chodron, *When Things Fall Apart: Heart Advice for Difficult Times* (Boston: Shambhala Press, 2000).

Sonia Choquette's book, *Your Heart's Desire: Instructions for Creating the Life You Really Want* (New York: Three Rivers Press, 1997).

Anthony De Mello, *The Way to Love* (New York: Image Books, 1995).

Eugene T. Gendlin, *Focusing* (New York: Bantam, 1982).

David Gregson & Jay S. Efran, *The Tao of Sobriety: Helping Your to Recover from Alcohol and Drug Addiction* (New York: St. Martin's Press, 2002).
C.G. Jung, *Memories, Dreams, Reflections* trans. Aniela Jaffe (New York: Vintage Press, 1989).

Thomas Kasulis, *Intimacy and Integrity: Philosophy and Cultural Difference* (Honolulu: University of Hawaii, 2002).

Geneen Roth, *When Food is Love: Exploring the Relationship between Food and Intimacy* (New York, Plume Press, 1993).

Philip Z., *A Skeptic's Guide to the 12 Steps* (Minneapolis: Hazelden, 1990).

www.ingramcontent.com/pod-product-compliance
Lightning Source LLC
Chambersburg PA
CBHW020000290326
41935CB00007B/250